MznLnx

Missing Links Exam Preps

Exam Prep for

Microeconomics

Perloff, 4th Edition

The MznLnx Exam Prep is your link from the texbook and lecture to your exams.
The MznLnx Exam Preps are unauthorized and comprehensive reviews of your textbooks.

All material provided by MznLnx and Rico Publications (c) 2010
Textbook publishers and textbook authors do not particpate in or contribute to these reviews.

MznLnx

Rico
Publications

Exam Prep for Microeconomics
4th Edition
Perloff

Publisher: Raymond Houge
Assistant Editor: Michael Rouger
Text and Cover Designer: Lisa Buckner
Marketing Manager: Sara Swagger
Project Manager, Editorial Production: Jerry Emerson
Art Director: Vernon Lowerui

Product Manager: Dave Mason
Editorial Assitant: Rachel Guzmanji
Pedagogy: Debra Long
Cover Image: Jim Reed/Getty Images
Text and Cover Printer: City Printing, Inc.
Compositor: Media Mix, Inc.

(c) 2010 Rico Publications
ALL RIGHTS RESERVED. No part of this work
covered by the copyright may be reproduced or
used in any form or by an means--graphic, electronic,
or mechanical, including photocopying, recording,
taping, Web distribution, information storage, and
retrieval systems, or in any other manner--without the
written permission of the publisher.

Printed in the United States
ISBN:

For more information about our products, contact us at:
Dave.Mason@RicoPublications.com

For permission to use material from this text or
product, submit a request online to:
Dave.Mason@RicoPublications.com

Contents

CHAPTER 1
Introduction — 1

CHAPTER 2
Supply and Demand — 5

CHAPTER 3
Applying the Supply-and-Demand Model — 12

CHAPTER 4
Consumer Choice — 18

CHAPTER 5
Applying Consumer Theory — 23

CHAPTER 6
Firms and Production — 32

CHAPTER 7
Costs — 39

CHAPTER 8
Competitive Firms and Markets — 51

CHAPTER 9
Applying the Competitive Model — 61

CHAPTER 10
General Equilibrium and Economic Welfare — 71

CHAPTER 11
Monopoly — 80

CHAPTER 12
Pricing — 89

CHAPTER 13
Oligopoly and Monopolistic Competition — 94

CHAPTER 14
Strategy — 107

CHAPTER 15
Factor Markets and Vertical Integration — 113

CHAPTER 16
Interest Rates, Investments, and Capital Markets — 123

CHAPTER 17
Uncertainty — 136

CHAPTER 18
Externalities, Open-Access, and Public Goods — 141

CHAPTER 19
Asymmetric Information — 152

CHAPTER 20
Contracts and Moral Hazards — 156

ANSWER KEY — 161

TO THE STUDENT

COMPREHENSIVE

The *MznLnx* Exam Prep series is designed to help you pass your exams. Editors at MznLnx review your textbooks and then prepare these practice exams to help you master the textbook material. Unlike study guides, workbooks, and practice tests provided by the texbook publisher and textbook authors, *MznLnx* gives you **all** of the material in each chapter in exam form, not just samples, so you can be sure to nail your exam.

MECHANICAL

The MznLnx Exam Prep series creates exams that will help you learn the subject matter as well as test you on your understanding. Each question is designed to help you master the concept. Just working through the exams, you gain an understanding of the subject--its a simple mechanical process that produces success.

INTEGRATED STUDY GUIDE AND REVIEW

MznLnx is not just a set of exams designed to test you, its also a comprehensive review of the subject content. Each exam question is also a review of the concept, making sure that you will get the answer correct without having to go to other sources of material. You learn as you go! Its the easiest way to pass an exam.

HUMOR

Studying can be tedious and dry. MznLnx's instructional design includes moderate humor within the exam questions on occassion, to break the tedium and revitalize the brain

Chapter 1. Introduction

1. _____ is a branch of economics that studies how individuals, households and firms and some states make decisions to allocate limited resources, typically in markets where goods or services are being bought and sold. _____ examines how these decisions and behaviours affect the supply and demand for goods and services, which determines prices; and how prices, in turn, determine the supply and demand of goods and services.

Whereas macroeconomics involves the 'sum total of economic activity, dealing with the issues of growth, inflation and unemployment, and with national economic policies relating to these issues' and the effects of government actions on them.

   a. Microeconomics   b. Countercyclical
   c. New Keynesian economics   d. Recession

2. _____ in economics and business is the result of an exchange and from that trade we assign a numerical monetary value to a good, service or asset. If Alice trades Bob 4 apples for an orange, the _____ of an orange is 4 apples. Inversely, the _____ of an apple is 1/4 oranges.

   a. Price war   b. Price book
   c. Premium pricing   d. Price

3. Applied microeconomics includes a range of specialized areas of study, many of which draw on methods from other fields. Applied work often uses little more than the basics of _____, supply and demand. Industrial organization and regulation examines topics such as the entry and exit of firms, innovation, role of trademarks.

   a. Price theory   b. Monopolistic competition
   c. Financial crises   d. Microeconomics

4. A _____ is a situation that involves losing one quality or aspect of something in return for gaining another quality or aspect. It implies a decision to be made with full comprehension of both the upside and downside of a particular choice.

In economics the term is expressed as opportunity cost, referring the most preferred alternative given up.

   a. Trade-off   b. Friedman-Savage utility function
   c. Whitemail   d. Nonmarket

5. In finance, a _____ is a debt security, in which the authorized issuer owes the holders a debt and, depending on the terms of the _____, is obliged to pay interest (the coupon) and/or to repay the principal at a later date, termed maturity. A _____ is a formal contract to repay borrowed money with interest at fixed intervals.

Thus a _____ is like a loan: the issuer is the borrower (debtor), the holder is the lender (creditor), and the coupon is the interest.

   a. Prize Bond   b. Callable
   c. Zero-coupon   d. Bond

6. _____ exists when sales of identical goods or services are transacted at different prices from the same provider. In a theoretical market with perfect information, no transaction costs or prohibition on secondary exchange (or re-selling) to prevent arbitrage, _____ can only be a feature of monopoly and oligopoly markets, where market power can be exercised. Otherwise, the moment the seller tries to sell the same good at different prices, the buyer at the lower price can arbitrage by selling to the consumer buying at the higher price but with a tiny discount.

a. Price discrimination
c. Transfer pricing
b. Lerner Index
d. Loss leader

7. _____ are costs incurred on the purchase of land, buildings, construction and equipment to be used in the production of goods or the rendering of services. In other words, the total cost needed to bring a project to a commercially operable status. However, _____ are not limited to the initial construction of a factory or other business.

a. Whitemail
c. Blanket order
b. Total revenue
d. Capital costs

8. In algebra, a _____ is a function depending on n that associates a scalar, det(A), to an n×n square matrix A. The fundamental geometric meaning of a _____ is a scale factor for measure when A is regarded as a linear transformation. _____s are important both in calculus, where they enter the substitution rule for several variables, and in multilinear algebra.

For a fixed nonnegative integer n, there is a unique _____ function for the n×n matrices over any commutative ring R. In particular, this function exists when R is the field of real or complex numbers.

a. 100-year flood
c. Determinant
b. 1921 recession
d. 130-30 fund

9. In economics, game theory, and decision theory the _____ theorem or _____ hypothesis predicts that the 'betting preferences' of people with regard to uncertain outcomes (gambles) can be described by a mathematical relation which takes into account the size of a payout (whether in money or other goods), the probability of occurrence, risk aversion, and the different utility of the same payout to people with different assets or personal preferences. It is a more sophisticated theory than simply predicting that choices will be made based on expected value (which takes into account only the size of the payout and the probability of occurrence.)

Daniel Bernoulli described the complete theory in 1738.

a. Ordinal utility
c. Expected utility
b. Expected utility hypothesis
d. Utility

10. In economics, _____ is a measure of the relative satisfaction from consumption of various goods and services. Given this measure, one may speak meaningfully of increasing or decreasing _____, and thereby explain economic behavior in terms of attempts to increase one's _____. For illustrative purposes, changes in _____ are sometimes expressed in units called utils.

a. Ordinal utility
c. Utility function
b. Expected utility hypothesis
d. Utility

11. An _____ is a tax based on the value of real estate or personal property. It is more common than the opposite, a specific duty, or a tax based on the quantity of an item regardless of price.

An _____ is typically imposed at the time of a transaction), but it may be imposed on an annual basis (real or personal property tax) or in connection with another significant event (inheritance tax, surrendering citizenship, or tariffs.)

| a. Optimal tax | b. Indirect tax |
| c. User charge | d. Ad valorem tax |

12. A _____ is a consumption tax charged at the point of purchase for certain goods and services. The tax is usually set as a percentage by the government charging the tax. There is usually a list of exemptions.

| a. 1921 recession | b. Sales tax |
| c. 130-30 fund | d. 100-year flood |

13. A _____ is a duty imposed on goods when they are moved across a political boundary. They are usually associated with protectionism, the economic policy of restraining trade between nations. For political reasons, _____s are usually imposed on imported goods, although they may also be imposed on exported goods.

| a. 100-year flood | b. Tariff |
| c. 130-30 fund | d. 1921 recession |

14. In economics, _____ is equal to total cost divided by the number of goods produced (the output quantity, Q.) It is also equal to the sum of average variable costs (total variable costs divided by Q) plus average fixed costs (total fixed costs divided by Q.) _____s may be dependent on the time period considered (increasing production may be expensive or impossible in the short term, for example.)

| a. Average variable cost | b. Average fixed cost |
| c. Explicit cost | d. Average cost |

15. In economics, a _____ is a graph of the costs of production as a function of total quantity produced. In a free market economy, productively efficient firms use these curves to find the optimal point of production, where they make the most profits. There are a few different types of _____s, each relevant to a different area of economics.

| a. Kuznets curve | b. Cost curve |
| c. Demand curve | d. Phillips curve |

16. To _____ is to impose a financial charge or other levy upon a taxpayer by a state or the functional equivalent of a state.

_____es are also imposed by many subnational entities. _____es consist of direct _____ or indirect _____, and may be paid in money or as its labour equivalent (often but not always unpaid.)

| a. Tax | b. 100-year flood |
| c. 1921 recession | d. 130-30 fund |

17. A _____ refers to property being sold by a taxing authority or the court to recover delinquent taxes.

When property taxes are not paid, title gets transferred to the state. The owner will then have a period of time to redeem the property by paying the overdue taxes, including penalties and costs.

| a. Tax competition | b. Tax wedge |
| c. Taxation as theft | d. Tax Sale |

18. To tax is to impose a financial charge or other levy upon a taxpayer by a state or the functional equivalent of a state.

_____ are also imposed by many subnational entities. _____ consist of direct tax or indirect tax, and may be paid in money or as its labour equivalent (often but not always unpaid.)

   a. 130-30 fund
   b. 1921 recession
   c. 100-year flood
   d. Taxes

19. _____s is the social science that studies the production, distribution, and consumption of goods and services. The term _____s comes from the Ancient Greek oá¼°κονομῖα from oá¼¶κος (oikos, 'house') + vĺŒμος (nomos, 'custom' or 'law'), hence 'rules of the house(hold)'. Current _____ models developed out of the broader field of political economy in the late 19th century, owing to a desire to use an empirical approach more akin to the physical sciences.
   a. Opportunity cost
   b. Inflation
   c. Energy economics
   d. Economic

20. In economics, a _____ expresses a judgement about whether a situation is desirable or undesirable. 'The world would be a better place if the moon were made of green cheese' is a _____ because it expresses a judgement about what ought to be. Notice that there is no way of disproving this statement.
   a. Market development funds
   b. Level playing field
   c. Market microstructure
   d. Normative statement

21. In economics and philosophy, a _____ concerns what is, and contains no indication of approval or disapproval. A _____ can be factually incorrect: 'The moon is made of black and gold cheese' is false, but a _____, as it is a statement about what exists. _____s are contrasted with normative statements.
   a. Whitemail
   b. Seasonally adjusted annual rate
   c. Race to the bottom
   d. Positive statement

22. The _____ is a group of three respected economists who advise the President of the United States on economic policy. It is a part of the Executive Office of the President of the United States, and provides much of the economic policy of the White House. The council prepares the annual Economic Report of the President.
   a. Constrained Pareto optimality
   b. Hybrid renewable energy systems
   c. Federal Reserve Bank Notes
   d. Council of Economic Advisers

Chapter 2. Supply and Demand

1. Economics:

    - _____, the desire to own something and the ability to pay for it
    - _____ curve, a graphic representation of a _____ schedule
    - _____ deposit, the money in checking accounts
    - _____ pull theory, the theory that inflation occurs when _____ for goods and services exceeds existing supplies
    - _____ schedule, a table that lists the quantity of a good a person will buy it each different price
    - _____ side economics, the school of economics at believes government spending and tax cuts open economy by raising _____

    a. Production
    b. McKesson ' Robbins scandal
    c. Variability
    d. Demand

2. An _____ is a tax levied on the financial income of people, corporations, or other legal entities. Various _____ systems exist, with varying degrees of tax incidence. Income taxation can be progressive, proportional, or regressive.

    a. AD-IA Model
    b. ACEA agreement
    c. ACCRA Cost of Living Index
    d. Income tax

3. In economics, economic equilibrium is simply a state of the world where economic forces are balanced and in the absence of external influences the (equilibrium) values of economic variables will not change. It is the point at which quantity demanded and quantity supplied are equal. _____, for example, refers to a condition where a market price is established through competition such that the amount of goods or services sought by buyers is equal to the amount of goods or services produced by sellers.

    a. Market equilibrium
    b. Marketization
    c. Regulated market
    d. Product-Market Growth Matrix

4. A _____ is a consumption tax charged at the point of purchase for certain goods and services. The tax is usually set as a percentage by the government charging the tax. There is usually a list of exemptions.

    a. 100-year flood
    b. Sales tax
    c. 1921 recession
    d. 130-30 fund

5. To _____ is to impose a financial charge or other levy upon a taxpayer by a state or the functional equivalent of a state.

    _____es are also imposed by many subnational entities. _____es consist of direct _____ or indirect _____, and may be paid in money or as its labour equivalent (often but not always unpaid.)

    a. 1921 recession
    b. 130-30 fund
    c. 100-year flood
    d. Tax

6. To tax is to impose a financial charge or other levy upon a taxpayer by a state or the functional equivalent of a state.

    _____ are also imposed by many subnational entities. _____ consist of direct tax or indirect tax, and may be paid in money or as its labour equivalent (often but not always unpaid.)

a. 1921 recession
b. 130-30 fund
c. 100-year flood
d. Taxes

7. The _____ is the market for securities, where companies and governments can raise longterm funds. It is a market in which money is lent for periods longer than a year. The _____ includes the stock market and the bond market.
   a. Performance attribution
   b. Multi-family office
   c. Financial instrument
   d. Capital market

8. In economics, a common-pool resource, alternatively termed a _____ resource, is a particular type of good consisting of a natural or human-made resource system, the size or characteristics of which makes it costly, but not impossible, to exclude potential beneficiaries from obtaining benefits from its use. Unlike pure public goods, common pool resources face problems of congestion or overuse, because they are subtractable. A common-pool resource typically consists of a core resource, which defines the stock variable, while providing a limited quantity of extractable fringe units, which defines the flow variable.
   a. Government monopoly
   b. Price-cap regulation
   c. Common-pool resource
   d. Common property

9. _____ is a broad label that refers to any individuals or households that use goods and services generated within the economy. The concept of a _____ is used in different contexts, so that the usage and significance of the term may vary.

Typically when business people and economists talk of _____s they are talking about person as _____, an aggregated commodity item with little individuality other than that expressed in the buy/not-buy decision.

   a. 100-year flood
   b. 130-30 fund
   c. 1921 recession
   d. Consumer

10. In economics, the _____ can be defined as the graph depicting the relationship between the price of a certain commodity, and the amount of it that consumers are willing and able to purchase at that given price. It is a graphic representation of a demand schedule. The _____ for all consumers together follows from the _____ of every individual consumer: the individual demands at each price are added together.
    a. Cost curve
    b. Kuznets curve
    c. Wage curve
    d. Demand curve

11. _____ in economics and business is the result of an exchange and from that trade we assign a numerical monetary value to a good, service or asset. If Alice trades Bob 4 apples for an orange, the _____ of an orange is 4 apples. Inversely, the _____ of an apple is 1/4 oranges.
    a. Premium pricing
    b. Price book
    c. Price war
    d. Price

12. In economics, _____ is equal to total cost divided by the number of goods produced (the output quantity, Q.) It is also equal to the sum of average variable costs (total variable costs divided by Q) plus average fixed costs (total fixed costs divided by Q.) _____s may be dependent on the time period considered (increasing production may be expensive or impossible in the short term, for example.)

a. Explicit cost
b. Average variable cost
c. Average fixed cost
d. Average cost

13. In economics, a _____ is a graph of the costs of production as a function of total quantity produced. In a free market economy, productively efficient firms use these curves to find the optimal point of production, where they make the most profits. There are a few different types of _____s, each relevant to a different area of economics.
   a. Phillips curve
   b. Demand curve
   c. Kuznets curve
   d. Cost curve

14. In economics, the _____ is an economic law that states that consumers buy more of a good when its price decreases and less when its price increases.

There are certain goods which do not follow this law. These include Veblen and Giffen goods

   a. Financial crisis
   b. Law of Demand
   c. Market failure
   d. Georgism

15. _____ exists when sales of identical goods or services are transacted at different prices from the same provider. In a theoretical market with perfect information, no transaction costs or prohibition on secondary exchange (or re-selling) to prevent arbitrage, _____ can only be a feature of monopoly and oligopoly markets, where market power can be exercised. Otherwise, the moment the seller tries to sell the same good at different prices, the buyer at the lower price can arbitrage by selling to the consumer buying at the higher price but with a tiny discount.
   a. Transfer pricing
   b. Loss leader
   c. Lerner Index
   d. Price discrimination

16. In political science and economics, the _____ or agency dilemma treats the difficulties that arise under conditions of incomplete and asymmetric information when a principal hires an agent, such as the problem that the two may not have the same interests, while the principal is, presumably, hiring the agent to pursue the interests of the former.

Various mechanisms may be used to try to align the interests of the agent with those of the principal, such as piece rates/commissions, profit sharing, efficiency wages, performance measurement (including financial statements), the agent posting a bond, or fear of firing. The _____ is found in most employer/employee relationships, for example, when stockholders hire top executives of corporations.

   a. 130-30 fund
   b. 1921 recession
   c. Principal-agent problem
   d. 100-year flood

8 *Chapter 2. Supply and Demand*

17. A _____ is:

   - Rewrite _____, in generative grammar and computer science
   - Standardization, a formal and widely-accepted statement, fact, definition, or qualification
   - Operation, a determinate _____ for performing a mathematical operation and obtaining a certain result (Mathematics, Logic)
     - Unary operation
     - Binary operation
   - _____ of inference, a function from sets of formulae to formulae (Mathematics, Logic)
   - _____ of thumb, principle with broad application that is not intended to be strictly accurate or reliable for every situation. Also often simply referred to as a _____
   - Moral, an atomic element of a moral code for guiding choices in human behavior
   - Heuristic, a quantized '_____' which shows a tendency or probability for successful function
   - A regulation, as in sports
   - A Production _____, as in computer science
   - Procedural law, a _____ set governing the application of laws to cases
     - A law, which may informally be called a '_____'
     - A court ruling, a decision by a court
   - In the U.S. Government, a regulation mandated by Congress, but written or expanded upon by the Executive Branch.
   - Norm (sociology), an informal but widely accepted _____, concept, truth, definition, or qualification (social norms, legal norms, coding norms)
   - Norm (philosophy), a kind of sentence or a reason to act, feel or believe
   - 'Rulership' is the concept of governance by a government:
     - Military _____, governance by a military body
     - Monastic _____, a collection of precepts that guides the life of monks or nuns in a religious order where the superior holds the place of Christ
   - Slide _____

   - '_____,' a song by Ayumi Hamasaki
   - '_____,' a song by rapper Nas
   - '_____s,' an album by the band The Whitest Boy Alive
   - _____s: Pyaar Ka Superhit Formula, a 2003 Bollywood film
   - ruler, an instrument for measuring lengths
   - _____, a component of an astrolabe, circumferator or similar instrument
   - The _____s, a bestselling self-help book
   - _____ Project (Run Up-to-date Linux Everywhere), a project that aims to use up-to-date Linux software on old PCs
   - _____ engine, a software system that helps managing business _____s
   - Ja _____, a hip hop artist
     - R.U.L.E., a 2005 greatest hits album by rapper Ja _____
   - '_____s,' a KMFDM song

a. Technocracy   b. Procter ' Gamble
c. Demand   d. Rule

Chapter 2. Supply and Demand

18. A _____ is a duty imposed on goods when they are moved across a political boundary. They are usually associated with protectionism, the economic policy of restraining trade between nations. For political reasons, _____s are usually imposed on imported goods, although they may also be imposed on exported goods.
    a. 100-year flood
    b. Tariff
    c. 1921 recession
    d. 130-30 fund

19. In economics, an _____ is any good (e.g. a commodity) or service brought into one country from another country in a legitimate fashion, typically for use in trade. It is a good that is brought in from another country for sale. _____ goods or services are provided to domestic consumers by foreign producers. An _____ in the receiving country is an export to the sending country.
    a. Economic integration
    b. Incoterms
    c. Import quota
    d. Import

20. In economics, _____ is when quantity demanded is more than quantity supplied. See Economic shortage.
    a. AD-IA Model
    b. ACCRA Cost of Living Index
    c. ACEA agreement
    d. Excess demand

21. In economics, _____ is when quantity supplied is more than quantity demanded. .
    a. Effective unemployment rate
    b. Economic Value Creation
    c. Illicit financial flows
    d. Excess supply

22. In economics, _____ refers to either

    1. a simplifying assumption made by the new classical school that markets always go to where the quantity supplied equals the quantity demanded; or
    2. the process of getting there via price adjustment.

A _____ price is the price of a good or service at which quantity supplied is equal to quantity demanded. Also called the equilibrium price.

In simple terms, this means that markets tend to move towards prices which balance the quantity supplied and the quantity demanded, such that the market will eventually be cleared of all surpluses and shortages (excess supply and demand.) The first version assumes that this process occurs instantaneously.

   a. Noise trader
   b. Market clearing
   c. Market data
   d. Market portfolio

23. A _____ is the lowest hourly, daily or monthly wage that employers may legally pay to employees or workers. Equivalently, it is the lowest wage at which workers may sell their labor. Although _____ laws are in effect in a great many jurisdictions, there are differences of opinion about the benefits and drawbacks of a _____.
    a. Minimum wage
    b. Permanent war economy
    c. Microfoundations
    d. Marginal propensity to consume

Chapter 2. Supply and Demand

24. In economics, a _____ 'purchase') is a market form in which only one buyer faces many sellers. It is an example of imperfect competition, similar to a monopoly, in which only one seller faces many buyers. As the only purchaser of a good or service, the 'monopsonist' may dictate terms to its suppliers in the same manner that a monopolist controls the market for its buyers.

   a. 130-30 fund
   b. 100-year flood
   c. 1921 recession
   d. Monopsony

25. A _____ is a government imposed limit on how high a price can be charged on a product. For a _____ to be effective, it must differ from the free market price. In the graph at right, the supply and demand curves intersect to determine the free-market quantity and price.

   a. Fire sale
   b. Price ceiling
   c. Product sabotage
   d. Pricing

26. In economics, _____ is the ratio of the percent change in one variable to the percent change in another variable. It is a tool for measuring the responsiveness of a function to changes in parameters in a relative way. Commonly analyzed are _____ of substitution, price and wealth.

   a. ACEA agreement
   b. Elasticity of demand
   c. ACCRA Cost of Living Index
   d. Elasticity

27. The underground economy or _____ is a market where all commerce is conducted without regard to taxation, law or regulations of trade. The term is also often known as the underdog, shadow economy, black economy, parallel economy or phantom trades.

In modern societies the underground economy covers a vast array of activities.

   a. Social market economy
   b. Market economy
   c. Protectionism
   d. Black market

28. _____ is the body of law which prohibits employers from hiring employees or workers for less than a given hourly, daily or monthly minimum wage. More than 90% of all countries have some kind of minimum wage legislation.

Until relatively recently, _____s were usually very tightly focused.

   a. Bankruptcy in Canada
   b. Home country control
   c. Minimum wage law
   d. Joint venture

29. A _____ is a government- or group-imposed limit on how low a price can be charged for a product. In order for a _____ to be effective, it must be greater than the equilibrium price. An ineffective _____, below equilibrium price.

A _____ can be set below the free-market equilibrium price.

   a. Price floor
   b. Flat rate
   c. Two-part tariff
   d. Price markdown

30. In labor economics, the _____ hypothesis argues that wages, at least in some markets, are determined by more than simply supply and demand. Specifically, it points to the incentive for managers to pay their employees more than the market-clearing wage in order to increase their productivity or efficiency. This increased labor productivity pays for the relatively higher wages.
- a. Exogenous growth model
- b. Earnings calls
- c. Efficiency wage
- d. Inflatable rats

31. _____ or economic opportunity loss is the value of the next best alternative foregone as the result of making a decision. _____ analysis is an important part of a company's decision-making processes but is not treated as an actual cost in any financial statement. The next best thing that a person can engage in is referred to as the _____ of doing the best thing and ignoring the next best thing to be done.
- a. Industrial organization
- b. Economic ideology
- c. Economic
- d. Opportunity cost

32. In economics and related disciplines, a _____ is a cost incurred in making an economic exchange. For example, most people, when buying or selling a stock, must pay a commission to their broker; that commission is a _____ of doing the stock deal. Or consider buying a banana from a store; to purchase the banana, your costs will be not only the price of the banana itself, but also the energy and effort it requires to find out which of the various banana products you prefer, where to get them and at what price, the cost of traveling from your house to the store and back, the time waiting in line, and the effort of the paying itself; the costs above and beyond the cost of the banana are the _____s.
- a. Sliding scale fees
- b. Transaction cost
- c. Cost allocation
- d. Cost of poor quality

33. A _____ is a counterfeit agreement among industries. It is an informal organization of producers that agree to coordinate prices and production. _____s usually occur in an oligopolistic industry, where there is a small number of sellers and usually involve homogeneous products.
- a. Shill
- b. 100-year flood
- c. Shanzhai
- d. Cartel

34. _____ is the transition of a national economy from monopoly control by groups of large businesses to a free market economy. This change rarely arises naturally, and is generally the result of regulation by a governing body.

A modern example of _____ is the economic restructuring of Germany after the fall of the Third Reich in 1945.

- a. Complementary monopoly
- b. Monopolization
- c. Decartelization
- d. Market power

Chapter 3. Applying the Supply-and-Demand Model

1. _____ in economics and business is the result of an exchange and from that trade we assign a numerical monetary value to a good, service or asset. If Alice trades Bob 4 apples for an orange, the _____ of an orange is 4 apples. Inversely, the _____ of an apple is 1/4 oranges.
   a. Price book
   b. Premium pricing
   c. Price
   d. Price war

2. _____ is a broad label that refers to any individuals or households that use goods and services generated within the economy. The concept of a _____ is used in different contexts, so that the usage and significance of the term may vary.

   Typically when business people and economists talk of _____s they are talking about person as _____, an aggregated commodity item with little individuality other than that expressed in the buy/not-buy decision.

   a. Consumer
   b. 1921 recession
   c. 130-30 fund
   d. 100-year flood

3. The term surplus is used in economics for several related quantities. The _____ is the amount that consumers benefit by being able to purchase a product for a price that is less than they would be willing to pay. The producer surplus is the amount that producers benefit by selling at a market price mechanism that is higher than they would be willing to sell for.
   a. Microeconomic reform
   b. Necessity good
   c. Consumer surplus
   d. Marginal rate of technical substitution

4. Economics:

   - _____,the desire to own something and the ability to pay for it
   - _____ curve,a graphic representation of a _____ schedule
   - _____ deposit, the money in checking accounts
   - _____ pull theory,the theory that inflation occurs when _____ for goods and services exceeds existing supplies
   - _____ schedule,a table that lists the quantity of a good a person will buy it each different price
   - _____ side economics,the school of economics at believes government spending and tax cuts open economy by raising _____

   a. Production
   b. Variability
   c. McKesson ' Robbins scandal
   d. Demand

5. In economics, the _____ can be defined as the graph depicting the relationship between the price of a certain commodity, and the amount of it that consumers are willing and able to purchase at that given price. It is a graphic representation of a demand schedule. The _____ for all consumers together follows from the _____ of every individual consumer: the individual demands at each price are added together.
   a. Cost curve
   b. Wage curve
   c. Demand curve
   d. Kuznets curve

6. _____ exists when sales of identical goods or services are transacted at different prices from the same provider. In a theoretical market with perfect information, no transaction costs or prohibition on secondary exchange (or re-selling) to prevent arbitrage, _____ can only be a feature of monopoly and oligopoly markets, where market power can be exercised. Otherwise, the moment the seller tries to sell the same good at different prices, the buyer at the lower price can arbitrage by selling to the consumer buying at the higher price but with a tiny discount.
   a. Loss leader
   b. Lerner Index
   c. Transfer pricing
   d. Price discrimination

7. _____ is defined as the measure of responsiveness in the quantity demanded for a commodity as a result of change in price of the same commodity. It is a measure of how consumers react to a change in price. In other words, it is percentage change in quantity demanded as per the percentage change in price of the same commodity.
   a. 100-year flood
   b. 130-30 fund
   c. Price elasticity of demand
   d. 1921 recession

8. In economics, the _____ is defined as a numerical measure of the responsiveness of the quantity supplied of product (A) to a change in price of product (A) alone. It is the measure of the way quantity supplied reacts to a change in price.

For example, if, in response to a 10% rise in the price of a good, the quantity supplied increases by 20%, the _____ would be 20%/10% = 2.

   a. Passive income
   b. Hedonimetry
   c. Demand shaping
   d. Price elasticity of supply

9. In economics, _____ is the ratio of the percent change in one variable to the percent change in another variable. It is a tool for measuring the responsiveness of a function to changes in parameters in a relative way. Commonly analyzed are _____ of substitution, price and wealth.
   a. Elasticity
   b. ACEA agreement
   c. Elasticity of demand
   d. ACCRA Cost of Living Index

10. Price _____ is defined as the measure of responsiveness in the quantity demanded for a commodity as a result of change in price of the same commodity. It is a measure of how consumers react to a change in price. In other words, it is percentage change in quantity demanded by the percentage change in price of the same commodity.
    a. ACEA agreement
    b. Elasticity
    c. Elasticity of demand
    d. ACCRA Cost of Living Index

11. In economics, a common-pool resource, alternatively termed a _____ resource, is a particular type of good consisting of a natural or human-made resource system, the size or characteristics of which makes it costly, but not impossible, to exclude potential beneficiaries from obtaining benefits from its use. Unlike pure public goods, common pool resources face problems of congestion or overuse, because they are subtractable. A common-pool resource typically consists of a core resource, which defines the stock variable, while providing a limited quantity of extractable fringe units, which defines the flow variable.

a. Price-cap regulation
b. Common-pool resource
c. Government monopoly
d. Common property

12. A _____ or labor union is an organization of workers who have banded together to achieve common goals in key areas and working conditions. The _____, through its leadership, bargains with the employer on behalf of union members (rank and file members) and negotiates labor contracts (Collective bargaining) with employers. This may include the negotiation of wages, work rules, complaint procedures, rules governing hiring, firing and promotion of workers, benefits, workplace safety and policies.
    a. Consumer goods
    b. Trade union
    c. Guaranteed investment contracts
    d. Case-Shiller Home Price Indices

13. In economics, _____ describes demand that is not very sensitive to a change in price.
    a. Export-led growth
    b. Effective unemployment rate
    c. Inelastic
    d. Inflation hedge

14. A _____ is an object whose consumption increases the utility of the consumer, for which the quantity demanded exceeds the quantity supplied at zero price. _____s are usually modeled as having diminishing marginal utility. The first individual purchase has high utility; the second has less.
    a. Pie method
    b. Merit good
    c. Composite good
    d. Good

15. In economics, the _____ of demand measures the responsiveness of the demand of a good to the change in the income of the people demanding the good. It is calculated as the ratio of the percent change in demand to the percent change in income. For example, if, in response to a 10% increase in income, the demand of a good increased by 20%, the _____ of demand would be 20%/10% = 2.
    a. ACCRA Cost of Living Index
    b. ACEA agreement
    c. AD-IA Model
    d. Income elasticity

16. _____ is a theory of microeconomics that relates preferences to consumer demand curves. The link between personal preferences, consumption, and the demand curve is one of the most complex relations in economics. Implicitly, economists assume that anything purchased will be consumed, unless the purchase is for a productive activity.
    a. Financial crisis
    b. Rational choice theory
    c. Consumer theory
    d. Literacy rate

17. In economics, the _____ measures the responsiveness of the demand of a good to the change in the income of the people demanding the good. It is calculated as the ratio of the percent change in demand to the percent change in income. For example, if, in response to a 10% increase in income, the demand of a good increased by 20%, the _____ would be 20%/10% = 2.
    a. Elasticity of substitution
    b. Income elasticity of Demand
    c. Expenditure minimization problem
    d. Indifference map

18. The _____ is the market for securities, where companies and governments can raise longterm funds. It is a market in which money is lent for periods longer than a year. The _____ includes the stock market and the bond market.
    a. Multi-family office
    b. Performance attribution
    c. Financial instrument
    d. Capital market

Chapter 3. Applying the Supply-and-Demand Model

19. In economic models, the _____ time frame assumes no fixed factors of production. Firms can enter or leave the marketplace, and the cost (and availability) of land, labor, raw materials, and capital goods can be assumed to vary. In contrast, in the short-run time frame, certain factors are assumed to be fixed, because there is not sufficient time for them to change.
   a. Diseconomies of scale
   b. Productivity world
   c. Price/performance ratio
   d. Long-run

20. In economics, the concept of the _____ refers to the decision-making time frame of a firm in which at least one factor of production is fixed. Costs which are fixed in the _____ have no impact on a firms decisions. For example a firm can raise output by increasing the amount of labour through overtime.
   a. Productivity model
   b. Product Pipeline
   c. Hicks-neutral technical change
   d. Short-run

21. In economics, _____ is equal to total cost divided by the number of goods produced (the output quantity, Q.) It is also equal to the sum of average variable costs (total variable costs divided by Q) plus average fixed costs (total fixed costs divided by Q.) _____s may be dependent on the time period considered (increasing production may be expensive or impossible in the short term, for example.)
   a. Average variable cost
   b. Average cost
   c. Average fixed cost
   d. Explicit cost

22. In economics, a _____ is a graph of the costs of production as a function of total quantity produced. In a free market economy, productively efficient firms use these curves to find the optimal point of production, where they make the most profits. There are a few different types of _____s, each relevant to a different area of economics.
   a. Demand curve
   b. Kuznets curve
   c. Phillips curve
   d. Cost curve

23. An _____ is a tax based on the value of real estate or personal property. It is more common than the opposite, a specific duty, or a tax based on the quantity of an item regardless of price.

   An _____ is typically imposed at the time of a transaction), but it may be imposed on an annual basis (real or personal property tax) or in connection with another significant event (inheritance tax, surrendering citizenship, or tariffs.)

   a. User charge
   b. Ad valorem tax
   c. Indirect tax
   d. Optimal tax

24. A _____ is a consumption tax charged at the point of purchase for certain goods and services. The tax is usually set as a percentage by the government charging the tax. There is usually a list of exemptions.
   a. 1921 recession
   b. Sales tax
   c. 100-year flood
   d. 130-30 fund

25. A _____ is a duty imposed on goods when they are moved across a political boundary. They are usually associated with protectionism, the economic policy of restraining trade between nations. For political reasons, _____s are usually imposed on imported goods, although they may also be imposed on exported goods.

Chapter 3. Applying the Supply-and-Demand Model

a. 130-30 fund
b. 100-year flood
c. 1921 recession
d. Tariff

26. To _____ is to impose a financial charge or other levy upon a taxpayer by a state or the functional equivalent of a state.

_____es are also imposed by many subnational entities. _____es consist of direct _____ or indirect _____, and may be paid in money or as its labour equivalent (often but not always unpaid.)

a. 100-year flood
b. 130-30 fund
c. 1921 recession
d. Tax

27. To tax is to impose a financial charge or other levy upon a taxpayer by a state or the functional equivalent of a state.

_____ are also imposed by many subnational entities. _____ consist of direct tax or indirect tax, and may be paid in money or as its labour equivalent (often but not always unpaid.)

a. Taxes
b. 1921 recession
c. 100-year flood
d. 130-30 fund

28. In economics, _____ is the analysis of the effect of a particular tax on the distribution of economic welfare. _____ is said to 'fall' upon the group that, at the end of the day, bears the burden of the tax. The key concept is that the _____ or tax burden does not depend on where the revenue is collected, but on the price elasticity of demand and price elasticity of supply.

a. 130-30 fund
b. 100-year flood
c. 1921 recession
d. Tax incidence

29. _____ are the income that is gained by governments because of taxation of the people.

Just as there are different types of tax, the form in which _____ is collected also differs; furthermore, the agency that collects the tax may not be part of central government, but may be an alternative third-party licenced to collect tax which they themselves will use. For example:

- In the UK, the DVLA collects road tax, which is then passed on the treasury.

_____s on purchases can come from two forms: 'tax' itself is a percentage of the price added to the purchase (such as sales tax in US states, or VAT in the UK), while 'duty' is a fixed amount added to the purchase price (such as is commonly found on cigarettes.) In order to calculate the total tax raised from these sales, we must work out the effective tax rate multiplied by the quantity supplied.

a. Tax revenue
b. Taxation as slavery
c. Tax and spend
d. Taxable wage

Chapter 3. Applying the Supply-and-Demand Model

30. In economics, a _____ is a loss of economic efficiency that can occur when equilibrium for a good or service is not Pareto optimal. In other words, either people who would have more marginal benefit than marginal cost are not buying the good or service, or people who would have more marginal cost than marginal benefit are buying the product.

Causes of _____ can include monopoly pricing, externalities, taxes or subsidies, and binding price ceilings or floors.

   a. Distributive efficiency
   b. Leapfrogging
   c. Contract curve
   d. Deadweight loss

31. A _____ refers to property being sold by a taxing authority or the court to recover delinquent taxes.

When property taxes are not paid, title gets transferred to the state. The owner will then have a period of time to redeem the property by paying the overdue taxes, including penalties and costs.

   a. Tax competition
   b. Tax Sale
   c. Tax wedge
   d. Taxation as theft

Chapter 4. Consumer Choice

1. _____ is a broad label that refers to any individuals or households that use goods and services generated within the economy. The concept of a _____ is used in different contexts, so that the usage and significance of the term may vary.

Typically when business people and economists talk of _____s they are talking about person as _____, an aggregated commodity item with little individuality other than that expressed in the buy/not-buy decision.

   a. 100-year flood
   b. 130-30 fund
   c. 1921 recession
   d. Consumer

2. A _____ represents the combinations of goods and services that a consumer can purchase given current prices and his income. Consumer theory uses the concepts of a _____ and a preference map to analyze consumer choices. Both concepts have a ready graphical representation in the two-good case.
   a. Revealed preference
   b. Quality bias
   c. Joint demand
   d. Budget constraint

3. A _____ is an object whose consumption increases the utility of the consumer, for which the quantity demanded exceeds the quantity supplied at zero price. _____s are usually modeled as having diminishing marginal utility. The first individual purchase has high utility; the second has less.
   a. Composite good
   b. Merit good
   c. Good
   d. Pie method

4. In microeconomic theory, an _____ is a graph showing different bundles of goods, each measured as to quantity, between which a consumer is indifferent. That is, at each point on the curve, the consumer has no preference for one bundle over another. In other words, they are all equally preferred.
   a. Expenditure minimization problem
   b. Indifference map
   c. Indifference curve
   d. Engel curve

5. In microeconomic theory a _____ or indifference map is the collection of indifference curves possessed by an individual. Similar in nature to a topographical map, the contour lines of such a map demonstrating progressively more desirable options as they move upward or to the right. Because of the nature of indifference curves they cannot intersect and are effectively infinite in number, their sum defining all possible combinations of values.
   a. Deferred gratification
   b. Cross elasticity of demand
   c. Marginal rate of substitution
   d. Preference map

6. In economics, the _____ is the rate at which a consumer is ready to give up one good in exchange for another good while maintaining the same level of satisfaction.

Under the standard assumption of neoclassical economics that goods and services are continuously divisible, the marginal rates of substitution will be the same regardless of the direction of exchange, and will correspond to the slope of an indifference curve (more precisely, to the slope multiplied by -1) passing through the consumption bundle in question, at that point: mathematically, it is the implicit derivative. MRS of Y for X is the amount of Y for which a consumer is willing to exchange for X locally.

a. Marginal rate of substitution
c. Quality bias
b. Supply and demand
d. Demand vacuum

7. In economics, _____ is a measure of the relative satisfaction from consumption of various goods and services. Given this measure, one may speak meaningfully of increasing or decreasing _____, and thereby explain economic behavior in terms of attempts to increase one's _____. For illustrative purposes, changes in _____ are sometimes expressed in units called utils.
   a. Utility function
   b. Expected utility hypothesis
   c. Ordinal utility
   d. Utility

8. While preferences are the conventional foundation of microeconomics, it is often convenient to represent preferences with a _____ and reason indirectly about preferences with _____s. Let X be the consumption set, the set of all mutually-exclusive packages the consumer could conceivably consume (such as an indifference curve map without the indifference curves.) The consumer's _____ $u : X \to \mathbf{R}$ ranks each package in the consumption set.
   a. Utility function
   b. Ordinal utility
   c. Utility
   d. Expected utility hypothesis

9. In economics, the _____ of a good or of a service is the utility of the specific use to which an agent would put a given increase in that good or service, or of the specific use that would be abandoned in response to a given decrease. In other words, _____ is the utility of the marginal use -- which, on the assumption of economic rationality, would be the least urgent use of the good or service, from the best feasible combination of actions in which its use is included. Under the mainstream assumptions, the _____ of a good or service is the posited quantified change in utility obtained by increasing or by decreasing use of that good or service.
   a. 1921 recession
   b. 100-year flood
   c. 130-30 fund
   d. Marginal utility

10. The slope of the production-possibility frontier (PPF) at any given point is called the _____ It describes numerically the rate at which one good can be transformed into the other. It is also called the (marginal) 'opportunity cost' of a commodity, that is, it is the opportunity cost of X in terms of Y at the margin.
    a. Fordism
    b. Piece work
    c. Productivity
    d. Marginal rate of transformation

11. _____ is a common concept in economics, and gives rise to derived concepts such as consumer debt. Generally _____ is defined by opposition to production. But the precise definition can vary because different schools of economists define production quite differently.
    a. Cash or share options
    b. Foreclosure data providers
    c. Federal Reserve Bank Notes
    d. Consumption

12. _____ in economics and business is the result of an exchange and from that trade we assign a numerical monetary value to a good, service or asset. If Alice trades Bob 4 apples for an orange, the _____ of an orange is 4 apples. Inversely, the _____ of an apple is 1/4 oranges.
    a. Price book
    b. Price war
    c. Price
    d. Premium pricing

Chapter 4. Consumer Choice

13. _____ refers to a business or organization attempting to acquire goods or services to accomplish the goals of the enterprise. Though there are several organizations that attempt to set standards in the _____ process, processes can vary greatly between organizations. Typically the word '_____' is not used interchangeably with the word 'procurement', since procurement typically includes Expediting, Supplier Quality, and Traffic and Logistics (T'L) in addition to _____.
   a. Purchasing
   b. Free port
   c. 100-year flood
   d. 130-30 fund

14. The term surplus is used in economics for several related quantities. The _____ is the amount that consumers benefit by being able to purchase a product for a price that is less than they would be willing to pay. The producer surplus is the amount that producers benefit by selling at a market price mechanism that is higher than they would be willing to sell for.
   a. Marginal rate of technical substitution
   b. Necessity good
   c. Microeconomic reform
   d. Consumer surplus

15. Economics:

   - _____, the desire to own something and the ability to pay for it
   - _____ curve, a graphic representation of a _____ schedule
   - _____ deposit, the money in checking accounts
   - _____ pull theory, the theory that inflation occurs when _____ for goods and services exceeds existing supplies
   - _____ schedule, a table that lists the quantity of a good a person will buy it each different price
   - _____ side economics, the school of economics at believes government spending and tax cuts open economy by raising _____

   a. Production
   b. Variability
   c. Demand
   d. McKesson ' Robbins scandal

16. The Court of Justice of the European Communities, usually called the _____, is the highest court in the European Union in matters of European Community law. It has the ultimate say on matters of EU law in order to ensure its equal application across all EU member states.

   The court was established in 1952 and is -- unlike most other Union institutions -- based in Luxembourg.

   a. ACCRA Cost of Living Index
   b. ACEA agreement
   c. European Union
   d. European Court of Justice

17. The _____ is an economic and political union of 27 member states, located primarily in Europe. It was established by the Treaty of Maastricht on 1 November 1993, upon the foundations of the pre-existing European Economic Community. With a population of almost 500 million, the _____ generates an estimated 30% share (US$18.4 trillion in 2008) of the nominal gross world product.
   a. ACEA agreement
   b. European Court of Justice
   c. European Union
   d. ACCRA Cost of Living Index

18. An _____ is a tax based on the value of real estate or personal property. It is more common than the opposite, a specific duty, or a tax based on the quantity of an item regardless of price.

Chapter 4. Consumer Choice

An _____ is typically imposed at the time of a transaction), but it may be imposed on an annual basis (real or personal property tax) or in connection with another significant event (inheritance tax, surrendering citizenship, or tariffs.)

   a. Indirect tax   b. Ad valorem tax
   c. Optimal tax   d. User charge

19. A _____ is a consumption tax charged at the point of purchase for certain goods and services. The tax is usually set as a percentage by the government charging the tax. There is usually a list of exemptions.

   a. 130-30 fund   b. 1921 recession
   c. Sales tax   d. 100-year flood

20. A _____ is a duty imposed on goods when they are moved across a political boundary. They are usually associated with protectionism, the economic policy of restraining trade between nations. For political reasons, _____s are usually imposed on imported goods, although they may also be imposed on exported goods.

   a. 130-30 fund   b. 100-year flood
   c. Tariff   d. 1921 recession

21. In economics, _____ is the ratio of the percent change in one variable to the percent change in another variable. It is a tool for measuring the responsiveness of a function to changes in parameters in a relative way. Commonly analyzed are _____ of substitution, price and wealth.

   a. ACEA agreement   b. Elasticity
   c. Elasticity of demand   d. ACCRA Cost of Living Index

22. To _____ is to impose a financial charge or other levy upon a taxpayer by a state or the functional equivalent of a state.

_____es are also imposed by many subnational entities. _____es consist of direct _____ or indirect _____, and may be paid in money or as its labour equivalent (often but not always unpaid.)

   a. 130-30 fund   b. 100-year flood
   c. 1921 recession   d. Tax

23. A _____ refers to property being sold by a taxing authority or the court to recover delinquent taxes.

When property taxes are not paid, title gets transferred to the state. The owner will then have a period of time to redeem the property by paying the overdue taxes, including penalties and costs.

   a. Tax Sale   b. Taxation as theft
   c. Tax wedge   d. Tax competition

24. To tax is to impose a financial charge or other levy upon a taxpayer by a state or the functional equivalent of a state.

_____ are also imposed by many subnational entities. _____ consist of direct tax or indirect tax, and may be paid in money or as its labour equivalent (often but not always unpaid.)

a. 130-30 fund
b. Taxes
c. 1921 recession
d. 100-year flood

Chapter 5. Applying Consumer Theory

1. _____ is a broad label that refers to any individuals or households that use goods and services generated within the economy. The concept of a _____ is used in different contexts, so that the usage and significance of the term may vary.

Typically when business people and economists talk of _____s they are talking about person as _____, an aggregated commodity item with little individuality other than that expressed in the buy/not-buy decision.

a. 130-30 fund
b. 1921 recession
c. Consumer
d. 100-year flood

2. A _____ is a measure of the average price of consumer goods and services purchased by households. A _____ measures a price change for a constant market basket of goods and services from one period to the next within the same area (city, region, or nation.) It is a price index determined by measuring the price of a standard group of goods meant to represent the typical market basket of a typical urban consumer.

a. Cost-of-living index
b. Lipstick index
c. CPI
d. Consumer Price Index

3. _____ is a theory of microeconomics that relates preferences to consumer demand curves. The link between personal preferences, consumption, and the demand curve is one of the most complex relations in economics. Implicitly, economists assume that anything purchased will be consumed, unless the purchase is for a productive activity.

a. Literacy rate
b. Financial crisis
c. Rational choice theory
d. Consumer theory

4. In economics, _____ is a rise in the general level of prices of goods and services in an economy over a period of time. When the general price level rises, each unit of currency buys fewer goods and services; consequently, _____ is also a decline in the real value of money--a loss of purchasing power in the medium of exchange which is also the monetary unit of account in the economy. A chief measure of general price-level _____ is the general _____ rate, which is the percentage change in a general price index (normally the Consumer Price Index) over time.

a. Inflation
b. Energy economics
c. Economic
d. Opportunity cost

5. _____ in economics and business is the result of an exchange and from that trade we assign a numerical monetary value to a good, service or asset. If Alice trades Bob 4 apples for an orange, the _____ of an orange is 4 apples. Inversely, the _____ of an apple is 1/4 oranges.

a. Price
b. Price war
c. Premium pricing
d. Price book

6. A _____ is a normalized average (typically a weighted average) of prices for a given class of goods or services in a given region, during a given interval of time. It is a statistic designed to help to compare how these prices, taken as a whole, differ between time periods or geographical locations.

Price indices have several potential uses.

a. Two-part tariff
b. Price Index
c. Product sabotage
d. Transactional Net Margin Method

Chapter 5. Applying Consumer Theory

7. _____ is a term used to described a tendency or preference towards a particular perspective, ideology or result, especially when the tendency interferes with the ability to be impartial, unprejudiced, or objective. The term _____ed is used to describe an action, judgment, or other outcome influenced by a prejudged perspective. It is also used to refer to a person or body of people whose actions or judgments exhibit _____.
   a. 1921 recession
   b. Bias
   c. 100-year flood
   d. 130-30 fund

8. Economics:

   - _____, the desire to own something and the ability to pay for it
   - _____ curve, a graphic representation of a _____ schedule
   - _____ deposit, the money in checking accounts
   - _____ pull theory, the theory that inflation occurs when _____ for goods and services exceeds existing supplies
   - _____ schedule, a table that lists the quantity of a good a person will buy it each different price
   - _____ side economics, the school of economics at believes government spending and tax cuts open economy by raising _____

   a. McKesson ' Robbins scandal
   b. Variability
   c. Production
   d. Demand

9. In economics, the _____ can be defined as the graph depicting the relationship between the price of a certain commodity, and the amount of it that consumers are willing and able to purchase at that given price. It is a graphic representation of a demand schedule. The _____ for all consumers together follows from the _____ of every individual consumer: the individual demands at each price are added together.
   a. Wage curve
   b. Kuznets curve
   c. Cost curve
   d. Demand curve

10. _____ is a common concept in economics, and gives rise to derived concepts such as consumer debt. Generally _____ is defined by opposition to production. But the precise definition can vary because different schools of economists define production quite differently.
    a. Consumption
    b. Foreclosure data providers
    c. Federal Reserve Bank Notes
    d. Cash or share options

11. _____ is a term in economics, where demand for one good or service occurs as a result of demand for another. This may occur as the former is a part of production of the second. For example, demand for coal leads to _____ for mining, as coal must be mined for coal to be consumed.
    a. Rate risk
    b. Derived demand
    c. Days Sales Outstanding
    d. Leontief production function

12. A _____ represents the combinations of goods and services that a consumer can purchase given current prices and his income. Consumer theory uses the concepts of a _____ and a preference map to analyze consumer choices. Both concepts have a ready graphical representation in the two-good case.

a. Budget constraint
b. Quality bias
c. Joint demand
d. Revealed preference

13. In economics, an _____ shows how the quantity demanded of a good or service changes as the consumer's income level changes. It is named after the 19th century German statistician Ernst Engel.

Graphically, the _____ is represented in the first-quadrant of the cartesian coordinate system.

a. Engel curve
b. Utility maximization problem
c. Expenditure minimization problem
d. Induced consumption

14. In economics, the _____ of demand measures the responsiveness of the demand of a good to the change in the income of the people demanding the good. It is calculated as the ratio of the percent change in demand to the percent change in income. For example, if, in response to a 10% increase in income, the demand of a good increased by 20%, the _____ of demand would be 20%/10% = 2.

a. ACCRA Cost of Living Index
b. ACEA agreement
c. AD-IA Model
d. Income elasticity

15. _____ is defined as the measure of responsiveness in the quantity demanded for a commodity as a result of change in price of the same commodity. It is a measure of how consumers react to a change in price. In other words, it is percentage change in quantity demanded as per the percentage change in price of the same commodity.

a. Price elasticity of demand
b. 1921 recession
c. 100-year flood
d. 130-30 fund

16. In economics, the _____ is defined as a numerical measure of the responsiveness of the quantity supplied of product (A) to a change in price of product (A) alone. It is the measure of the way quantity supplied reacts to a change in price.

For example, if, in response to a 10% rise in the price of a good, the quantity supplied increases by 20%, the _____ would be 20%/10% = 2.

a. Demand shaping
b. Passive income
c. Hedonimetry
d. Price elasticity of supply

17. In economics, _____ is the ratio of the percent change in one variable to the percent change in another variable. It is a tool for measuring the responsiveness of a function to changes in parameters in a relative way. Commonly analyzed are _____ of substitution, price and wealth.

a. Elasticity of demand
b. Elasticity
c. ACCRA Cost of Living Index
d. ACEA agreement

18. Price _____ is defined as the measure of responsiveness in the quantity demanded for a commodity as a result of change in price of the same commodity. It is a measure of how consumers react to a change in price. In other words, it is percentage change in quantity demanded by the percentage change in price of the same commodity.

a. Elasticity of demand
c. Elasticity
b. ACEA agreement
d. ACCRA Cost of Living Index

19. In consumer theory, an _____ is a good that decreases in demand when consumer income rises, unlike normal goods, for which the opposite is observed. It is a good that consumers demand increases when their income increases. Inferiority, in this sense, is an observable fact relating to affordability rather than a statement about the quality of the good.
   a. Independent goods
   c. Information good
   b. Inferior good
   d. Export-oriented

20. In economics, _____s are any goods for which demand increases when income increases and falls when income decreases but price remains constant, i.e. with a positive income elasticity of demand. The term does not necessarily refer to the quality of the good.

Depending on the indifference curves, the amount of a good bought can either increase, decrease, or stay the same when income increases.

   a. Normative economics
   c. Bord halfpenny
   b. Financial contagion
   d. Normal good

21. _____ exists when sales of identical goods or services are transacted at different prices from the same provider. In a theoretical market with perfect information, no transaction costs or prohibition on secondary exchange (or re-selling) to prevent arbitrage, _____ can only be a feature of monopoly and oligopoly markets, where market power can be exercised. Otherwise, the moment the seller tries to sell the same good at different prices, the buyer at the lower price can arbitrage by selling to the consumer buying at the higher price but with a tiny discount.
   a. Transfer pricing
   c. Lerner Index
   b. Loss leader
   d. Price discrimination

22. A _____ is a price discrimination technique in which the price of a product or service is composed of two parts - a lump-sum fee as well as a per-unit charge. In general, price discrimination techniques only occur in partially or fully monopolistic markets. It is designed to enable the firm to capture more consumer surplus than it otherwise would in a non-discriminating pricing environment.
   a. Price floor
   c. Penetration pricing
   b. Big ticket item
   d. Two-part tariff

23. A _____ is an object whose consumption increases the utility of the consumer, for which the quantity demanded exceeds the quantity supplied at zero price. _____s are usually modeled as having diminishing marginal utility. The first individual purchase has high utility; the second has less.
   a. Good
   c. Pie method
   b. Composite good
   d. Merit good

24. A _____ is a duty imposed on goods when they are moved across a political boundary. They are usually associated with protectionism, the economic policy of restraining trade between nations. For political reasons, _____s are usually imposed on imported goods, although they may also be imposed on exported goods.
   a. 1921 recession
   c. 130-30 fund
   b. 100-year flood
   d. Tariff

Chapter 5. Applying Consumer Theory

25. An _____ is a tax based on the value of real estate or personal property. It is more common than the opposite, a specific duty, or a tax based on the quantity of an item regardless of price.

An _____ is typically imposed at the time of a transaction), but it may be imposed on an annual basis (real or personal property tax) or in connection with another significant event (inheritance tax, surrendering citizenship, or tariffs.)

 a. Indirect tax
 b. Ad valorem tax
 c. User charge
 d. Optimal tax

26. A _____ is a consumption tax charged at the point of purchase for certain goods and services. The tax is usually set as a percentage by the government charging the tax. There is usually a list of exemptions.

 a. 100-year flood
 b. Sales tax
 c. 1921 recession
 d. 130-30 fund

27. To _____ is to impose a financial charge or other levy upon a taxpayer by a state or the functional equivalent of a state.

_____es are also imposed by many subnational entities. _____es consist of direct _____ or indirect _____, and may be paid in money or as its labour equivalent (often but not always unpaid.)

 a. 1921 recession
 b. Tax
 c. 100-year flood
 d. 130-30 fund

28. To tax is to impose a financial charge or other levy upon a taxpayer by a state or the functional equivalent of a state.

_____ are also imposed by many subnational entities. _____ consist of direct tax or indirect tax, and may be paid in money or as its labour equivalent (often but not always unpaid.)

 a. 1921 recession
 b. 100-year flood
 c. 130-30 fund
 d. Taxes

29. In economics, a _____ is a loss of economic efficiency that can occur when equilibrium for a good or service is not Pareto optimal. In other words, either people who would have more marginal benefit than marginal cost are not buying the good or service, or people who would have more marginal cost than marginal benefit are buying the product.

Causes of _____ can include monopoly pricing, externalities, taxes or subsidies, and binding price ceilings or floors.

 a. Leapfrogging
 b. Contract curve
 c. Distributive efficiency
 d. Deadweight loss

30. A _____ refers to property being sold by a taxing authority or the court to recover delinquent taxes.

Chapter 5. Applying Consumer Theory

When property taxes are not paid, title gets transferred to the state. The owner will then have a period of time to redeem the property by paying the overdue taxes, including penalties and costs.

a. Taxation as theft
b. Tax competition
c. Tax wedge
d. Tax Sale

31. In economics, the _____ is the change in consumption resulting from a change in real income.

Another important item that can change is the money income of the consumer. The _____ is the phenomenon observed through changes in purchasing power.

a. Equilibrium wage
b. Export subsidy
c. Income effect
d. Inflation hedge

32. The _____ in economics relates changes in Marshallian demand to changes in Hicksian demand. It demonstrates that demand changes due to price changes are a result of two effects:

- a substitution effect, the result of a change in the exchange rate between two goods; and
- an income effect, the effect of price results in a change of the consumer's purchasing power.

Each element of the Slutsky matrix is given by

$$\frac{\partial x_i(p,w)}{\partial p_j} = \frac{\partial h_i(p,u)}{\partial p_j} - \frac{\partial x_i(p,w)}{\partial w} x_j(p,w),$$

where h(p,u) is the Hicksian demand and x(p,w) is the Marshallian demand, at price level p, wealth level w, and utility level u. The first term represents the substitution effect, and the second term represents the income effect.

The same equation can be rewritten in matrix form and is called the Slutsky matrix

$$D_p x(p,w) = D_p h(p,u) - D_w x(p,w) x(p,w)^\top,$$

where D_p is the derivative operator with respect to price and D_w is the derivative operator with respect to wealth.

a. 100-year flood
b. 130-30 fund
c. Simultaneous equations
d. Slutsky equation

33. The term surplus is used in economics for several related quantities. The _____ is the amount that consumers benefit by being able to purchase a product for a price that is less than they would be willing to pay. The producer surplus is the amount that producers benefit by selling at a market price mechanism that is higher than they would be willing to sell for.

Chapter 5. Applying Consumer Theory

a. Microeconomic reform
b. Necessity good
c. Marginal rate of technical substitution
d. Consumer surplus

34. _____ refers to a business or organization attempting to acquire goods or services to accomplish the goals of the enterprise. Though there are several organizations that attempt to set standards in the _____ process, processes can vary greatly between organizations. Typically the word '_____' is not used interchangeably with the word 'procurement', since procurement typically includes Expediting, Supplier Quality, and Traffic and Logistics (T'L) in addition to _____.

a. 130-30 fund
b. Free port
c. Purchasing
d. 100-year flood

35. _____ is the number of goods/services that can be purchased with a unit of currency. For example, if you had taken one dollar to a store in the 1950s, you would have been able to buy a greater number of items than you would today, indicating that you would have had a greater _____ in the 1950s. Currency can be either a commodity money, like gold or silver, or fiat currency like US dollars.

a. Genuine progress indicator
b. Compliance cost
c. Human Poverty Index
d. Purchasing power

36. In economics and consumer theory, a _____ is one which people consume more of as price rises, violating the law of demand. In normal situations, as the price of such a good rises, the substitution effect causes people to purchase less of it and more of substitute goods. In the _____ situation, cheaper close substitutes are not available.

a. Demerit good
b. Giffen good
c. Search good
d. Pie method

37. In economics, the _____ is an economic law that states that consumers buy more of a good when its price decreases and less when its price increases.

There are certain goods which do not follow this law. These include Veblen and Giffen goods

a. Georgism
b. Financial crisis
c. Market failure
d. Law of Demand

38. _____ is the process of adjusting economic indicators and the prices of goods and services from different time periods to the same price level. To adjust for inflation, an indicator is divided by the inflation index.

It is easy to show that 7% inflation, lasting 10 years, would nearly double the cost of living (1.0710=1.96.)

a. Investment goods
b. Inflation adjustment
c. Alternative employment arrangements
d. International Marketmakers Combination

39. _____ describes a bias in gay economics index numbers arising from tendency to purchase inexpensive substitutes for expensive items when prices change.

_____ occurs when two or more items experience a change of price relative to each other. Consumers will consume more of the now comparatively inexpensive good and less of the now relatively more expensive good.

a. Market basket
b. Constant dollars
c. State of World Liberty Index
d. Substitution bias

40. The _____, a unit of the United States Department of Labor, is the principal fact-finding agency for the U.S. government in the broad field of labor economics and statistics. The BLS is an independent national statistical agency that collects, processes, analyzes, and disseminates essential statistical data to the American public, the U.S. Congress, other Federal agencies, State and local governments, business, and labor representatives. The BLS also serves as a statistical resource to the Department of Labor.
   a. Gross national product
   b. Gross Regional Product
   c. Gross world product
   d. Bureau of Labor Statistics

41. The supply of labor is the number of total hours that workers wish to work at a given real wage rate.

    _____ curves are derived from the 'labor-leisure' trade-off. More hours worked earn higher incomes but necessitate a cut in the amount of leisure that workers enjoy.

   a. Late capitalism
   b. Creative capitalism
   c. Human trafficking
   d. Labor supply

42. In microeconomic theory, an _____ is a graph showing different bundles of goods, each measured as to quantity, between which a consumer is indifferent. That is, at each point on the curve, the consumer has no preference for one bundle over another. In other words, they are all equally preferred.
   a. Indifference map
   b. Expenditure minimization problem
   c. Engel curve
   d. Indifference curve

43. _____ is an online peer-reviewed magazine published by the Agricultural ' Applied Economics Association (AAEA) for readers interested in the policy and management of agriculture, the food industry, natural resources, rural communities, and the environment. _____ is published quarterly and is available free online. It is currently one of three outreach products offered by AAEA, along with the more timely Policy Issues and the forthcoming Shared Materials section of the AAEA Web site.
   a. 100-year flood
   b. 130-30 fund
   c. 1921 recession
   d. Choices

44. In economics, _____ is equal to total cost divided by the number of goods produced (the output quantity, Q.) It is also equal to the sum of average variable costs (total variable costs divided by Q) plus average fixed costs (total fixed costs divided by Q.) _____s may be dependent on the time period considered (increasing production may be expensive or impossible in the short term, for example.)
   a. Average variable cost
   b. Average cost
   c. Explicit cost
   d. Average fixed cost

45. In economics, a _____ is a graph of the costs of production as a function of total quantity produced. In a free market economy, productively efficient firms use these curves to find the optimal point of production, where they make the most profits. There are a few different types of _____s, each relevant to a different area of economics.
   a. Phillips curve
   b. Cost curve
   c. Demand curve
   d. Kuznets curve

Chapter 5. Applying Consumer Theory

46. _____s is the social science that studies the production, distribution, and consumption of goods and services. The term _____s comes from the Ancient Greek οἰκονομία from οἶκος (oikos, 'house') + νόμος (nomos, 'custom' or 'law'), hence 'rules of the house(hold)'. Current _____ models developed out of the broader field of political economy in the late 19th century, owing to a desire to use an empirical approach more akin to the physical sciences.
   a. Energy economics
   b. Inflation
   c. Economic
   d. Opportunity cost

47. An _____ is a tax levied on the financial income of people, corporations, or other legal entities. Various _____ systems exist, with varying degrees of tax incidence. Income taxation can be progressive, proportional, or regressive.
   a. ACEA agreement
   b. AD-IA Model
   c. ACCRA Cost of Living Index
   d. Income tax

48. _____ are the income that is gained by governments because of taxation of the people.

Just as there are different types of tax, the form in which _____ is collected also differs; furthermore, the agency that collects the tax may not be part of central government, but may be an alternative third-party licenced to collect tax which they themselves will use. For example:

- In the UK, the DVLA collects road tax, which is then passed on the treasury.

_____s on purchases can come from two forms: 'tax' itself is a percentage of the price added to the purchase (such as sales tax in US states, or VAT in the UK), while 'duty' is a fixed amount added to the purchase price (such as is commonly found on cigarettes.) In order to calculate the total tax raised from these sales, we must work out the effective tax rate multiplied by the quantity supplied.

   a. Tax and spend
   b. Taxable wage
   c. Taxation as slavery
   d. Tax revenue

Chapter 6. Firms and Production

1. The _____ consists of a number of economic theories which describe the nature of the firm, company including its existence, its behaviour, and its relationship with the market.

In simplified terms, the _____ aims to answer these questions:

1. Existence - why do firms emerge, why are not all transactions in the economy mediated over the market?
2. Boundaries - why the boundary between firms and the market is located exactly there? Which transactions are performed internally and which are negotiated on the market?
3. Organization - why are firms structured in such specific way? What is the interplay of formal and informal relationships?

Despite looking simple, these questions are not answered by the established economic theory, which usually views firms as given, and treats them as black boxes without any internal structure.

The First World War period saw a change of emphasis in economic theory away from industry-level analysis which mainly included analysing markets to analysis at the level of the firm, as it became increasingly clear that perfect competition was no longer an adequate model of how firms behaved. Economic theory till then had focussed on trying to understand markets alone and there had been little study on understanding why firms or organisations exist.

a. Policy Ineffectiveness Proposition
b. Technology gap
c. Khazzoom-Brookes postulate
d. Theory of the firm

2. A _____ is a type of business entity in which partners (owners) share with each other the profits or losses of the business _____s are often favored over corporations for taxation purposes, as the _____ structure does not generally incur a tax on profits before it is distributed to the partners (i.e. there is no dividend tax levied.) However, depending on the _____ structure and the jurisdiction in which it operates, owners of a _____ may be exposed to greater personal liability than they would as shareholders of a corporation.

For a country-by-country listing of types of _____s, companies, etc., see Types of business entity.

a. Minimum wage law
b. Feoffee
c. Partnership
d. Due diligence

3. A mutual _____ or stockholder is an individual or company (including a corporation) that legally owns one or more shares of stock in a joint stock company. A company's _____s collectively own that company. Thus, the typical goal of such companies is to enhance _____ value.

a. Prime Standard
b. Relative valuation
c. Profit warning
d. Shareholder

4. A _____, or simply proprietorship is a type of business entity which legally has no separate existence from its owner. Hence, the limitations of liability enjoyed by a corporation and limited liability partnerships do not apply to sole proprietors. All debts of the business are debts of the owner.

a. Golden hello
b. Corporate tax
c. Golden parachute
d. Sole proprietorship

Chapter 6. Firms and Production

5. _____ is the term denoting either an entrance or changes which are inserted into a system and which activate/modify a process. It is an abstract concept, used in the modeling, system(s) design and system(s) exploitation. It is usually connected with other terms, e.g., _____ field, _____ variable, _____ parameter, _____ value, _____ signal, _____ device and _____ file.

- a. AD-IA Model
- b. Input
- c. ACCRA Cost of Living Index
- d. ACEA agreement

6. _____ is a concept whereby a person's financial liability is limited to a fixed sum, most commonly the value of a person's investment in a company or partnership with _____. A shareholder in a limited company is not personally liable for any of the debts of the company, other than for the value of his investment in that company. The same is true for the members of a _____ partnership and the limited partners in a limited partnership.

- a. Limited liability
- b. Deficiency judgment
- c. Personal Responsibility and Work Opportunity Reconciliation Act of 1996
- d. Nexus of contracts

7. _____s is the social science that studies the production, distribution, and consumption of goods and services. The term _____s comes from the Ancient Greek οἰκονομῖα from οἶκος (oikos, 'house') + νόμος (nomos, 'custom' or 'law'), hence 'rules of the house(hold)'. Current _____ models developed out of the broader field of political economy in the late 19th century, owing to a desire to use an empirical approach more akin to the physical sciences.

- a. Opportunity cost
- b. Inflation
- c. Energy economics
- d. Economic

8. In economics, the _____ functional form of production functions is widely used to represent the relationship of an output to inputs. It was proposed by Knut Wicksell (1851-1926), and tested against statistical evidence by Charles Cobb and Paul Douglas in 1900-1928.

For production, the function is

$$Y = AL^{\alpha}K^{\beta},$$

where:

- Y = total production (the monetary value of all goods produced in a year)
- L = labor input
- K = capital input
- A = total factor productivity
- α and β are the output elasticities of labor and capital, respectively. These values are constants determined by available technology.

Output elasticity measures the responsiveness of output to a change in levels of either labor or capital used in production, ceteris paribus. For example if $\alpha = 0.15$, a 1% increase in labor would lead to approximately a 0.15% increase in output.

Chapter 6. Firms and Production

a. Cobb-Douglas
b. Social savings
c. Demand-pull theory
d. Growth accounting

9. In microeconomics, _____ is quite simply the conversion of inputs into outputs. It is an economic process that uses resources to create a good or service that is suitable for exchange. This can include manufacturing, storing, shipping, and packaging.
a. Production
b. MET
c. Solved
d. Red Guards

10. In economics, a _____ is a function that specifies the output of a firm, an industry, or an entire economy for all combinations of inputs. A meta-_____ compares the practice of the existing entities converting inputs X into output y to determine the most efficient practice _____ of the existing entities, whether the most efficient feasible practice production or the most efficient actual practice production. In either case, the maximum output of a technologically-determined production process is a mathematical function of input factors of production.
a. Short-run
b. Constant elasticity of substitution
c. Production function
d. Post-Fordism

11. A _____ is a counterfeit agreement among industries. It is an informal organization of producers that agree to coordinate prices and production. _____s usually occur in an oligopolistic industry, where there is a small number of sellers and usually involve homogeneous products.
a. 100-year flood
b. Shill
c. Shanzhai
d. Cartel

12. _____ is the transition of a national economy from monopoly control by groups of large businesses to a free market economy. This change rarely arises naturally, and is generally the result of regulation by a governing body.

A modern example of _____ is the economic restructuring of Germany after the fall of the Third Reich in 1945.

a. Complementary monopoly
b. Monopolization
c. Market power
d. Decartelization

13. In economics, a _____ or a hard good is a good which does not quickly wear out it yields services or utility over time rather than being completely used up when used once. Most goods are therefore _____s to a certain degree. These are goods that can last for a relatively long time, such as refrigerators, cars, and DVD players.
a. Search good
b. Luxury good
c. Superior goods
d. Durable good

14. A _____ is an object whose consumption increases the utility of the consumer, for which the quantity demanded exceeds the quantity supplied at zero price. _____s are usually modeled as having diminishing marginal utility. The first individual purchase has high utility; the second has less.
a. Composite good
b. Merit good
c. Good
d. Pie method

Chapter 6. Firms and Production

15. The term _____, 'the state or characteristic of being variable',_____ describes how spread out or closely clustered a set of data is. may be applied to many different subjects:

- Climate _____
- Genetic _____
- Heart rate _____
- Human _____
- Solar van
- Spatial _____
- Statistical _____
- _____

a. Demand
b. Characteristic
c. Total product
d. Variability

16. In economics, the _____ or marginal physical product is the extra output produced by one more unit of an input (for instance, the difference in output when a firm's labour is increased from five to six units.) Assuming that no other inputs to production change, the _____ of a given input (X) can be expressed as:

_____ = ΔY/ΔX = (the change of Y)/(the change of X.)

-
  -
    - Pending approval by Thomas Sowell***

In neoclassical economics, this is the mathematical derivative of the production function.... Note that the 'product' (Y) is typically defined ignoring external costs and benefits.

a. Labor problem
b. Factor prices
c. Productive capacity
d. Marginal product

17. In economics, the _____ also known as MPL or MPN is the change in output from hiring one additional unit of labor. It is the increase in output added by the last unit of labor. Assuming that no other inputs to production change, the marginal product of a given input (X) can be expressed as:

MP = ΔY/ΔX = (the change of Y)/(the change of X.)

a. Marginal product of labor
b. Production function
c. Marginal product
d. Product Pipeline

18. In economics, the concept of the _____ refers to the decision-making time frame of a firm in which at least one factor of production is fixed. Costs which are fixed in the _____ have no impact on a firms decisions. For example a firm can raise output by increasing the amount of labour through overtime.

Chapter 6. Firms and Production

a. Product Pipeline
c. Productivity model
b. Hicks-neutral technical change
d. Short-run

19. The _____ of a variable factor of Production identifies what outputs are possible using various levels of the variable input. This can be displayed in either a chart that lists the output level corresponding to various levels of input, or a graph that summarizes the data into a '_____ curve'. The diagram shows a typical _____ curve. In this example, output increases as more inputs are employed up until point A. The maximum output possible with this Production process is Qm. (If there are other inputs used in the process, they are assumed to be fixed).
    a. Total product
    c. Tightness
    b. Consequence
    d. Convexity

20. In economics, _____ is the process by which a firm determines the price and output level that returns the greatest profit. There are several approaches to this problem. The total revenue--total cost method relies on the fact that profit equals revenue minus cost, and the marginal revenue--marginal cost method is based on the fact that total profit in a perfectly competitive market reaches its maximum point where marginal revenue equals marginal cost.
    a. Normal profit
    c. Profit maximization
    b. 100-year flood
    d. Profit margin

21. This concept is also known as the law of diminishing marginal returns, the _____, or the law of increasing opportunity cost.

The concept of diminishing returns can be traced back to the concerns of early economists such as Johann Heinrich von Thünen, Turgot, Thomas Malthus and David Ricardo.

Suppose that one kilogram of seed applied to a plot of land of a fixed size produces one ton of crop.

    a. Bennett Amendment
    c. Lang Law
    b. Fair Labor Standards Act
    d. Law of increasing relative cost

22. In economics, _____ refers to how the marginal contribution of a factor of production usually decreases as more of the factor is used. According to this relationship, in a production system with fixed and variable inputs, beyond some point, each additional unit of the variable input yields smaller and smaller increases in output. Conversely, producing one more unit of output costs more and more in variable inputs.
    a. Community property
    c. Patent troll
    b. Derivatives law
    d. Diminishing returns

23. _____ usually refers to the transformation of agriculture that began in 1945. One significant factor in this revolution was the Mexican government's request to establish an agricultural research station to develop more varieties of wheat that could be used to feed the rapidly growing population of the country.

In 1943, Mexico imported half its wheat, but by 1956, the _____ had made Mexico self-sufficient; by 1964, Mexico exported half a million tons of wheat.

    a. 100-year flood
    c. 1921 recession
    b. 130-30 fund
    d. Green Revolution

Chapter 6. Firms and Production

24. _____ in economics refers to metrics and measures of output from production processes, per unit of input. Labor _____, for example, is typically measured as a ratio of output per labor-hour, an input. _____ may be conceived of as a metrics of the technical or engineering efficiency of production.
    a. Productivity
    b. Fordism
    c. Piece work
    d. Production-possibility frontier

25. In economics, an _____ is a contour line drawn through the set of points at which the same quantity of output is produced while changing the quantities of two or more inputs. While an indifference curve helps to answer the utility-maximizing problem of consumers, the _____ deals with the cost-minimization problem of producers. _____s are typically drawn on capital-labor graphs, showing the tradeoff between capital and labor in the production function, and the decreasing marginal returns of both inputs.
    a. Isoquant
    b. Economic production quantity
    c. Economies of scale
    d. Underinvestment employment relationship

26. In economic models, the _____ time frame assumes no fixed factors of production. Firms can enter or leave the marketplace, and the cost (and availability) of land, labor, raw materials, and capital goods can be assumed to vary. In contrast, in the short-run time frame, certain factors are assumed to be fixed, because there is not sufficient time for them to change.
    a. Diseconomies of scale
    b. Price/performance ratio
    c. Long-run
    d. Productivity world

27. In microeconomic theory, an _____ is a graph showing different bundles of goods, each measured as to quantity, between which a consumer is indifferent. That is, at each point on the curve, the consumer has no preference for one bundle over another. In other words, they are all equally preferred.
    a. Expenditure minimization problem
    b. Indifference map
    c. Engel curve
    d. Indifference curve

28. A _____ represents the combinations of goods and services that a consumer can purchase given current prices and his income. Consumer theory uses the concepts of a _____ and a preference map to analyze consumer choices. Both concepts have a ready graphical representation in the two-good case.
    a. Budget constraint
    b. Quality bias
    c. Revealed preference
    d. Joint demand

29. In production, returns to scale refers to changes in output subsequent to a proportional change in all inputs (where all inputs increase by a constant factor.) If output increases by that same proportional change then there are _____ If output increases by less than that proportional change, there are decreasing returns to scale (DRS.)
    a. Lexicographic preferences
    b. Consumer sovereignty
    c. Long term
    d. Constant returns to scale

30. In calculus, a function f defined on a subset of the real numbers with real values is called _____, if for all x and y such that x >≤ y one has f(x) >≤ f(y), so f preserves the order. In layman's terms, the sign of the slope is always positive (the curve tending upwards) or zero (i.e., non-decreasing, or asymptotic, or depicted as a horizontal, flat line) Likewise, a function is called monotonically decreasing (non-increasing) if, whenever x >≤ y, then f(x) >≥ f(y), so it reverses the order.
    a. 100-year flood
    b. 1921 recession
    c. 130-30 fund
    d. Monotonic

Chapter 6. Firms and Production

31. In economics, _____ and economies of scale are related terms that describe what happens as the scale of production increases. They are different terms and should not be used interchangeably.

_____ refers to a technical property of production that examines changes in output subsequent to a proportional change in all inputs (where all inputs increase by a constant factor.)

   a. Necessity good
   b. Constant returns to scale
   c. Returns to scale
   d. Customer equity

32. _____ is a term that is used to describe the overall process of invention, innovation and diffusion of technology or processes. The term is redundant with technological development, technological achievement, and technological progress. In essence _____ is the invention of a technology (or a process), the continuous process of improving a technology (in which it often becomes cheaper) and its diffusion throughout industry or society.
   a. 130-30 fund
   b. 100-year flood
   c. 1921 recession
   d. Technological change

33. _____ was the American founder of the Ford Motor Company and father of modern assembly lines used in mass production. His introduction of the Model T automobile revolutionized transportation and American industry. He was a prolific inventor and was awarded 161 U.S. patents.
   a. Henry Ford
   b. Werner Sombart
   c. George Cabot Lodge II
   d. Maximilian Carl Emil Weber

34. _____ are conceptually similar to economies of scale. Whereas economies of scale primarily refer to efficiencies associated with supply-side changes, such as increasing or decreasing the scale of production, of a single product type, _____ refer to efficiencies primarily associated with demand-side changes, such as increasing or decreasing the scope of marketing and distribution, of different types of products. _____ are one of the main reasons for such marketing strategies as product bundling, product lining, and family branding.
   a. Isoquant
   b. Economic production quantity
   c. Economies of scale
   d. Economies of scope

Chapter 7. Costs

1. A _____ is an object whose consumption increases the utility of the consumer, for which the quantity demanded exceeds the quantity supplied at zero price. _____s are usually modeled as having diminishing marginal utility. The first individual purchase has high utility; the second has less.
    a. Composite good
    b. Pie method
    c. Merit good
    d. Good

2. _____ or economic opportunity loss is the value of the next best alternative foregone as the result of making a decision. _____ analysis is an important part of a company's decision-making processes but is not treated as an actual cost in any financial statement. The next best thing that a person can engage in is referred to as the _____ of doing the best thing and ignoring the next best thing to be done.
    a. Industrial organization
    b. Economic
    c. Economic ideology
    d. Opportunity cost

3. In microeconomics, _____ is quite simply the conversion of inputs into outputs. It is an economic process that uses resources to create a good or service that is suitable for exchange. This can include manufacturing, storing, shipping, and packaging.
    a. Solved
    b. Red Guards
    c. MET
    d. Production

4. _____ are costs incurred on the purchase of land, buildings, construction and equipment to be used in the production of goods or the rendering of services. In other words, the total cost needed to bring a project to a commercially operable status. However, _____ are not limited to the initial construction of a factory or other business.
    a. Blanket order
    b. Whitemail
    c. Total revenue
    d. Capital costs

5. In economic models, the _____ time frame assumes no fixed factors of production. Firms can enter or leave the marketplace, and the cost (and availability) of land, labor, raw materials, and capital goods can be assumed to vary. In contrast, in the short-run time frame, certain factors are assumed to be fixed, because there is not sufficient time for them to change.
    a. Diseconomies of scale
    b. Productivity world
    c. Price/performance ratio
    d. Long-run

6. In economics, the concept of the _____ refers to the decision-making time frame of a firm in which at least one factor of production is fixed. Costs which are fixed in the _____ have no impact on a firms decisions. For example a firm can raise output by increasing the amount of labour through overtime.
    a. Productivity model
    b. Product Pipeline
    c. Short-run
    d. Hicks-neutral technical change

7. _____s is the social science that studies the production, distribution, and consumption of goods and services. The term _____s comes from the Ancient Greek οἰκονομία from οἶκος (oikos, 'house') + νόμος (nomos, 'custom' or 'law'), hence 'rules of the house(hold)'. Current _____ models developed out of the broader field of political economy in the late 19th century, owing to a desire to use an empirical approach more akin to the physical sciences.
    a. Energy economics
    b. Opportunity cost
    c. Economic
    d. Inflation

8. The _____ of a decision depends on both the cost of the alternative chosen and the benefit that the best alternative would have provided if chosen. _____ differs from accounting cost because it includes opportunity cost.

Chapter 7. Costs

a. Economic Cost
b. Isocost
c. Epstein-Zin preferences
d. Inventory analysis

9. In economics, _____ is equal to total cost divided by the number of goods produced (the output quantity, Q.) It is also equal to the sum of average variable costs (total variable costs divided by Q) plus average fixed costs (total fixed costs divided by Q.) _____s may be dependent on the time period considered (increasing production may be expensive or impossible in the short term, for example.)

a. Average variable cost
b. Explicit cost
c. Average fixed cost
d. Average cost

10. In economics, a _____ is a graph of the costs of production as a function of total quantity produced. In a free market economy, productively efficient firms use these curves to find the optimal point of production, where they make the most profits. There are a few different types of _____s, each relevant to a different area of economics.

a. Phillips curve
b. Cost curve
c. Kuznets curve
d. Demand curve

11. In economics, a _____ or a hard good is a good which does not quickly wear out it yields services or utility over time rather than being completely used up when used once. Most goods are therefore _____s to a certain degree. These are goods that can last for a relatively long time, such as refrigerators, cars, and DVD players.

a. Superior goods
b. Luxury good
c. Durable good
d. Search good

12. In economics and business decision-making, _____ are costs that cannot be recovered once they have been incurred. _____ are sometimes contrasted with variable costs, which are the costs that will change due to the proposed course of action, and prospective costs which are costs that will be incurred if an action is taken.

In traditional microeconomic theory, only variable costs are relevant to a decision.

a. Post-purchase rationalization
b. Halo effect
c. Hyperbolic discounting
d. Sunk costs

13. In accounting, _____ is the original monetary value of an economic item. In some circumstances, assets and liabilities may be shown at their _____, as if there had been no change in value since the date of acquisition. The balance sheet value of the item may therefore differ from the 'true' value.

a. Deferred financing costs
b. Salvage value
c. Historical Cost
d. Net income per employee

14. _____ is a broad label that refers to any individuals or households that use goods and services generated within the economy. The concept of a _____ is used in different contexts, so that the usage and significance of the term may vary.

Typically when business people and economists talk of _____s they are talking about person as _____, an aggregated commodity item with little individuality other than that expressed in the buy/not-buy decision.

a. 1921 recession
b. 100-year flood
c. 130-30 fund
d. Consumer

15. The term surplus is used in economics for several related quantities. The _____ is the amount that consumers benefit by being able to purchase a product for a price that is less than they would be willing to pay. The producer surplus is the amount that producers benefit by selling at a market price mechanism that is higher than they would be willing to sell for.
  a. Necessity good
  b. Marginal rate of technical substitution
  c. Consumer surplus
  d. Microeconomic reform

16. In economics, _____ are business expenses that are not dependent on the activities of the business They tend to be time-related, such as salaries or rents being paid per month. This is in contrast to variable costs, which are volume-related (and are paid per quantity.)

In management accounting, _____ are defined as expenses that do not change in proportion to the activity of a business, within the relevant period or scale of production.

  a. Cost of poor quality
  b. Quality costs
  c. Cost-Volume-Profit Analysis
  d. Fixed costs

17. In economics, and cost accounting, _____ describes the total economic cost of production and is made up of variable costs, which vary according to the quantity of a good produced and include inputs such as labor and raw materials, plus fixed costs, which are independent of the quantity of a good produced and include inputs (capital) that cannot be varied in the short term, such as buildings and machinery. _____ in economics includes the total opportunity cost of each factor of production in addition to fixed and variable costs.

The rate at which _____ changes as the amount produced changes is called marginal cost.

  a. 1921 recession
  b. 130-30 fund
  c. 100-year flood
  d. Total cost

18. _____s are expenses that change in proportion to the activity of a business. In other words, _____ is the sum of marginal costs. It can also be considered normal costs.
  a. Quality costs
  b. Cost allocation
  c. Cost-Volume-Profit Analysis
  d. Variable cost

19. In economics and finance, _____ is the change in total cost that arises when the quantity produced changes by one unit. It is the cost of producing one more unit of a good. Mathematically, the _____ function is expressed as the first derivative of the total cost (TC) function with respect to quantity (Q.)
  a. Variable cost
  b. Khozraschyot
  c. Quality costs
  d. Marginal cost

20. A _____ is a counterfeit agreement among industries. It is an informal organization of producers that agree to coordinate prices and production. _____s usually occur in an oligopolistic industry, where there is a small number of sellers and usually involve homogeneous products.

Chapter 7. Costs

a. Shill
b. Shanzhai
c. 100-year flood
d. Cartel

21. _____ is the transition of a national economy from monopoly control by groups of large businesses to a free market economy. This change rarely arises naturally, and is generally the result of regulation by a governing body.

A modern example of _____ is the economic restructuring of Germany after the fall of the Third Reich in 1945.

a. Complementary monopoly
b. Monopolization
c. Market power
d. Decartelization

22. _____ is an economics term to describe a firms variable costs (labor, electricity, etc.) divided by the quantity (Q) of total units of output.

$$\mathrm{AVC} = \frac{\mathrm{TVC}}{Q}$$

Where:

- TVC = Total Variable Cost
- _____ = Average variable cost
- Q = Quantity of Units Produced

_____ plus average fixed cost equals average total cost:

_____ + AFC = ATC.

a. Inventory valuation
b. Average fixed cost
c. Average variable cost
d. Explicit cost

23. In economics, the _____ functional form of production functions is widely used to represent the relationship of an output to inputs. It was proposed by Knut Wicksell (1851-1926), and tested against statistical evidence by Charles Cobb and Paul Douglas in 1900-1928.

For production, the function is

$Y = AL^{\alpha}K^{\beta}$,

where:

- Y = total production (the monetary value of all goods produced in a year)
- L = labor input
- K = capital input
- A = total factor productivity
- α and β are the output elasticities of labor and capital, respectively. These values are constants determined by available technology.

Output elasticity measures the responsiveness of output to a change in levels of either labor or capital used in production, ceteris paribus. For example if α = 0.15, a 1% increase in labor would lead to approximately a 0.15% increase in output.

a. Demand-pull theory
c. Cobb-Douglas
b. Social savings
d. Growth accounting

24. In economics, a _____ is a function that specifies the output of a firm, an industry, or an entire economy for all combinations of inputs. A meta-_____ compares the practice of the existing entities converting inputs X into output y to determine the most efficient practice _____ of the existing entities, whether the most efficient feasible practice production or the most efficient actual practice production. In either case, the maximum output of a technologically-determined production process is a mathematical function of input factors of production.

a. Post-Fordism
c. Production function
b. Constant elasticity of substitution
d. Short-run

25. The _____ of a variable factor of Production identifies what outputs are possible using various levels of the variable input. This can be displayed in either a chart that lists the output level corresponding to various levels of input, or a graph that summarizes the data into a '_____ curve'. The diagram shows a typical _____ curve. In this example, output increases as more inputs are employed up until point A. The maximum output possible with this Production process is Qm. (If there are other inputs used in the process, they are assumed to be fixed).

a. Tightness
c. Convexity
b. Consequence
d. Total product

26. An _____ is a tax based on the value of real estate or personal property. It is more common than the opposite, a specific duty, or a tax based on the quantity of an item regardless of price.

An _____ is typically imposed at the time of a transaction), but it may be imposed on an annual basis (real or personal property tax) or in connection with another significant event (inheritance tax, surrendering citizenship, or tariffs.)

a. Indirect tax
c. Ad valorem tax
b. Optimal tax
d. User charge

27. A _____ is a consumption tax charged at the point of purchase for certain goods and services. The tax is usually set as a percentage by the government charging the tax. There is usually a list of exemptions.

44   *Chapter 7. Costs*

    a. 100-year flood   b. 1921 recession
    c. 130-30 fund   d. Sales tax

28. A _____ is a duty imposed on goods when they are moved across a political boundary. They are usually associated with protectionism, the economic policy of restraining trade between nations. For political reasons, _____s are usually imposed on imported goods, although they may also be imposed on exported goods.

    a. 100-year flood   b. 130-30 fund
    c. 1921 recession   d. Tariff

29. To _____ is to impose a financial charge or other levy upon a taxpayer by a state or the functional equivalent of a state.

_____es are also imposed by many subnational entities. _____es consist of direct _____ or indirect _____, and may be paid in money or as its labour equivalent (often but not always unpaid.)

    a. 100-year flood   b. 130-30 fund
    c. 1921 recession   d. Tax

30. A _____ refers to property being sold by a taxing authority or the court to recover delinquent taxes.

When property taxes are not paid, title gets transferred to the state. The owner will then have a period of time to redeem the property by paying the overdue taxes, including penalties and costs.

    a. Tax Sale   b. Tax competition
    c. Tax wedge   d. Taxation as theft

31. To tax is to impose a financial charge or other levy upon a taxpayer by a state or the functional equivalent of a state.

_____ are also imposed by many subnational entities. _____ consist of direct tax or indirect tax, and may be paid in money or as its labour equivalent (often but not always unpaid.)

    a. 100-year flood   b. 130-30 fund
    c. 1921 recession   d. Taxes

32. _____ is a tax charged by some US states to corporations formed in those states based on the number of shares they issue or, in some cases, the amount of their assets. The purpose of the tax is to raise revenue for the state. The State of Delaware has a significant _____, while other states, such as Nevada, have none at all or a smaller one.

    a. Tax reform   b. Tax policy
    c. Franchise tax   d. Current use

33. Under the system of feudalism, a _____, fief, feud, feoff often consisted of inheritable lands or revenue-producing property granted by a liege lord, generally to a vassal, in return for a form of allegiance, originally to give him the means to fulfill his military duties when called upon. However anything of value could be held in fief, such as an office, a right of exploitation (e.g., hunting, fishing) or any other type of revenue, rather than the land it comes from.

Originally, the feudal institution of vassalage did not imply the giving or receiving of landholdings (which were granted only as a reward for loyalty), but by the eighth century the giving of a landholding was becoming standard.

a. 100-year flood
b. Fiefdom
c. 1921 recession
d. 130-30 fund

34. _____ is the term denoting either an entrance or changes which are inserted into a system and which activate/modify a process. It is an abstract concept, used in the modeling, system(s) design and system(s) exploitation. It is usually connected with other terms, e.g., _____ field, _____ variable, _____ parameter, _____ value, _____ signal, _____ device and _____ file.

a. Input
b. ACCRA Cost of Living Index
c. ACEA agreement
d. AD-IA Model

35. In economics an _____ line represents a combination of inputs which all cost the same amount. Although similar to the budget constraint in consumer theory, the use of the _____ pertains to cost-minimization in production, as opposed to utility-maximization. The typical _____ line represents the ratio of costs of labour and capital, so the formula is often written as:

$$rK + wL = C$$

Where w represents the wage of labour, and r represents the rental rate of capital.

a. Inventory analysis
b. Epstein-Zin preferences
c. Isocost
d. Incentive

36. In economics, an _____ is a contour line drawn through the set of points at which the same quantity of output is produced while changing the quantities of two or more inputs. While an indifference curve helps to answer the utility-maximizing problem of consumers, the _____ deals with the cost-minimization problem of producers. _____s are typically drawn on capital-labor graphs, showing the tradeoff between capital and labor in the production function, and the decreasing marginal returns of both inputs.

a. Underinvestment employment relationship
b. Economic production quantity
c. Economies of scale
d. Isoquant

37. _____ is used to refer to a number of related concepts. It is the using resources in such a way as to maximize the production of goods and services. A system can be called economically efficient if:

- No one can be made better off without making someone else worse off.
- More output cannot be obtained without increasing the amount of inputs.
- Production proceeds at the lowest possible per-unit cost.

These definitions of efficiency are not equivalent, but they are all encompassed by the idea that nothing more can be achieved given the resources available.

An economic system is more efficient if it can provide more goods and services for society without using more resources.

a. ACEA agreement
b. ACCRA Cost of Living Index
c. Economic Efficiency
d. Efficient contract theory

38. In economics, the _____ or the Technical Rate of Substitution (TRS) is the amount by which the quantity of one input has to be reduced ($-\Delta x_2$) when one extra unit of another input is used ($\Delta x_1 = 1$), so that output remains constant ($y = \bar{y}$.)

$$MRTS(x_1, x_2) = \frac{\Delta x_2}{\Delta x_1} = -\frac{MP_1}{MP_2}$$

where MP_1 and MP_2 are the marginal products of input 1 and input 2, respectively.

Along an isoquant, the MRTS shows the rate at which one input (e.g. capital or labor) may be substituted for another, while maintaining the same level of output.

a. Household production function
b. Producer surplus
c. Marginal rate of technical substitution
d. Pork cycle

Chapter 7. Costs

39. A _____ is:

- Rewrite _____, in generative grammar and computer science
- Standardization, a formal and widely-accepted statement, fact, definition, or qualification
- Operation, a determinate _____ for performing a mathematical operation and obtaining a certain result (Mathematics, Logic)
    - Unary operation
    - Binary operation
- _____ of inference, a function from sets of formulae to formulae (Mathematics, Logic)
- _____ of thumb, principle with broad application that is not intended to be strictly accurate or reliable for every situation. Also often simply referred to as a _____
- Moral, an atomic element of a moral code for guiding choices in human behavior
- Heuristic, a quantized '_____' which shows a tendency or probability for successful function
- A regulation, as in sports
- A Production _____, as in computer science
- Procedural law, a _____ set governing the application of laws to cases
    - A law, which may informally be called a '_____'
    - A court ruling, a decision by a court
- In the U.S. Government, a regulation mandated by Congress, but written or expanded upon by the Executive Branch.
- Norm (sociology), an informal but widely accepted _____, concept, truth, definition, or qualification (social norms, legal norms, coding norms)
- Norm (philosophy), a kind of sentence or a reason to act, feel or believe
- 'Rulership' is the concept of governance by a government:
    - Military _____, governance by a military body
    - Monastic _____, a collection of precepts that guides the life of monks or nuns in a religious order where the superior holds the place of Christ
- Slide _____

- '_____,' a song by Ayumi Hamasaki
- '_____,' a song by rapper Nas
- '_____s,' an album by the band The Whitest Boy Alive
- _____s: Pyaar Ka Superhit Formula, a 2003 Bollywood film
- ruler, an instrument for measuring lengths
- _____, a component of an astrolabe, circumferator or similar instrument
- The _____s, a bestselling self-help book
- _____ Project (Run Up-to-date Linux Everywhere), a project that aims to use up-to-date Linux software on old PCs
- _____ engine, a software system that helps managing business _____s
- Ja _____, a hip hop artist
    - R.U.L.E., a 2005 greatest hits album by rapper Ja _____
- '_____s,' a KMFDM song

a. Procter ' Gamble
b. Technocracy
c. Rule
d. Demand

40. _____ are the prices that the factors of production of a finished item attract.

Chapter 7. Costs

There has been some economic debate as to what determines these prices. Classical and Marxist economists argued that the _____ decided the value of a product and so value was intrinsic within the product.

a. Productivity model
c. Marginal product of labor
b. Marginal product
d. Factor prices

41. _____ in economics and business is the result of an exchange and from that trade we assign a numerical monetary value to a good, service or asset. If Alice trades Bob 4 apples for an orange, the _____ of an orange is 4 apples. Inversely, the _____ of an apple is 1/4 oranges.

a. Premium pricing
c. Price war
b. Price book
d. Price

42. _____ is subcontracting a process, such as product design or manufacturing, to a third-party company. The decision to outsource is often made in the interest of lowering cost or making better use of time and energy costs, redirecting or conserving energy directed at the competencies of a particular business, or to make more efficient use of land, labor, capital, (information) technology and resources. _____ became part of the business lexicon during the 1980s.

a. Averch-Johnson effect
c. Electronic business
b. Additional Funds Needed
d. Outsourcing

43. In economics, a common-pool resource, alternatively termed a _____ resource, is a particular type of good consisting of a natural or human-made resource system, the size or characteristics of which makes it costly, but not impossible, to exclude potential beneficiaries from obtaining benefits from its use. Unlike pure public goods, common pool resources face problems of congestion or overuse, because they are subtractable. A common-pool resource typically consists of a core resource, which defines the stock variable, while providing a limited quantity of extractable fringe units, which defines the flow variable.

a. Common property
c. Price-cap regulation
b. Common-pool resource
d. Government monopoly

44. _____ are the forces that cause larger firms to produce goods and services at increased per-unit costs. They are less well known than what economists have long understood as 'economies of scale', the forces which enable larger firms to produce goods and services at reduced per-unit costs.

Some of the forces which cause a diseconomy of scale are listed below:

Ideally, all employees of a firm would have one-on-one communication with each other so they know exactly what the other workers are doing.

a. Marginal physical product
c. Diseconomies of scale
b. Factors of production
d. Productive capacity

45. _____, in microeconomics, are the cost advantages that a business obtains due to expansion. They are factors that cause a producere;s average cost per unit to fall as scale is increased. _____ is a long run concept and refers to reductions in unit cost as the size of a facility, or scale, increases.

a. Economic production quantity
b. Underinvestment employment relationship
c. Isoquant
d. Economies of scale

46. In economics, _____ and economies of scale are related terms that describe what happens as the scale of production increases. They are different terms and should not be used interchangeably.

_____ refers to a technical property of production that examines changes in output subsequent to a proportional change in all inputs (where all inputs increase by a constant factor.)

a. Necessity good
b. Customer equity
c. Returns to scale
d. Constant returns to scale

47. The _____ consists of a number of economic theories which describe the nature of the firm, company including its existence, its behaviour, and its relationship with the market.

In simplified terms, the _____ aims to answer these questions:

1. Existence - why do firms emerge, why are not all transactions in the economy mediated over the market?
2. Boundaries - why the boundary between firms and the market is located exactly there? Which transactions are performed internally and which are negotiated on the market?
3. Organization - why are firms structured in such specific way? What is the interplay of formal and informal relationships?

Despite looking simple, these questions are not answered by the established economic theory, which usually views firms as given, and treats them as black boxes without any internal structure.

The First World War period saw a change of emphasis in economic theory away from industry-level analysis which mainly included analysing markets to analysis at the level of the firm, as it became increasingly clear that perfect competition was no longer an adequate model of how firms behaved. Economic theory till then had focussed on trying to understand markets alone and there had been little study on understanding why firms or organisations exist.

a. Technology gap
b. Khazzoom-Brookes postulate
c. Policy Ineffectiveness Proposition
d. Theory of the firm

48. _____ are conceptually similar to economies of scale. Whereas economies of scale primarily refer to efficiencies associated with supply-side changes, such as increasing or decreasing the scale of production, of a single product type, _____ refer to efficiencies primarily associated with demand-side changes, such as increasing or decreasing the scope of marketing and distribution, of different types of products. _____ are one of the main reasons for such marketing strategies as product bundling, product lining, and family branding.

a. Economies of scope
b. Economies of scale
c. Economic production quantity
d. Isoquant

49. In economics, _____ refers to the ability of a person or a country to produce a particular good at a lower marginal cost and opportunity cost than another person or country. It is the ability to produce a product most efficiently given all the other products that could be produced. It can be contrasted with absolute advantage which refers to the ability of a person or a country to produce a particular good at a lower absolute cost than another.

    a. Hot money   b. Gravity model of trade
    c. Triffin dilemma   d. Comparative advantage

Chapter 8. Competitive Firms and Markets

1. In economics, _____ describes the state of a market with respect to competition.

   - Perfect competition, in which the market consists of a very large number of firms producing a homogeneous product.
   - Monopolistic competition where there are a large number of independent firms which have a very small proportion of the market share.
   - Oligopoly, in which a market is dominated by a small number of firms which own more than 40% of the market share.
   - Oligopsony, a market dominated by many sellers and a few buyers.
   - Monopoly, where there is only one provider of a product or service.
   - Natural monopoly, a monopoly in which economies of scale cause efficiency to increase continuously with the size of the firm. A firm is a natural monopoly if it is able to serve the entire market demand at a lower cost than any combination of two or more smaller, more specialized firms.
   - Monopsony, when there is only one buyer in a market.

   The imperfectly competitive structure is quite identical to the realistic market conditions where some monopolistic competitors, monopolists, oligopolists, and duopolists exist and dominate the market conditions. The elements of _____ include the number and size distribution of firms, entry conditions, and the extent of differentiation.

   These somewhat abstract concerns tend to determine some but not all details of a specific concrete market system where buyers and sellers actually meet and commit to trade.

   a. Human capital
   c. Labour economics
   b. Market structure
   d. Monopolistic competition

2. In economics, _____ is the process by which a firm determines the price and output level that returns the greatest profit. There are several approaches to this problem. The total revenue--total cost method relies on the fact that profit equals revenue minus cost, and the marginal revenue--marginal cost method is based on the fact that total profit in a perfectly competitive market reaches its maximum point where marginal revenue equals marginal cost.

   a. Profit margin
   c. 100-year flood
   b. Profit maximization
   d. Normal profit

3. In economics, _____ is equal to total cost divided by the number of goods produced (the output quantity, Q.) It is also equal to the sum of average variable costs (total variable costs divided by Q) plus average fixed costs (total fixed costs divided by Q.) _____s may be dependent on the time period considered (increasing production may be expensive or impossible in the short term, for example.)

   a. Average fixed cost
   c. Average cost
   b. Explicit cost
   d. Average variable cost

Chapter 8. Competitive Firms and Markets

4. _____ has several particular meanings:

- in mathematics
    - _____ function
    - Euler _____
    - _____
    - _____ subgroup
    - method of _____s (partial differential equations)
- in physics and engineering
    - any _____ curve that shows the relationship between certain input- and output parameters, e.g.
    - an I-V or current-voltage _____ is the current in a circuit as a function of the applied voltage
    - Receiver-Operator _____
- in fiction
    - in Dungeons ' Dragons, _____ is another name for ability score

a. Russian financial crisis
b. Demand
c. Technocracy
d. Characteristic

5. In economics, a _____ is a graph of the costs of production as a function of total quantity produced. In a free market economy, productively efficient firms use these curves to find the optimal point of production, where they make the most profits. There are a few different types of _____s, each relevant to a different area of economics.

a. Demand curve
b. Phillips curve
c. Kuznets curve
d. Cost curve

6. _____s is the social science that studies the production, distribution, and consumption of goods and services. The term _____s comes from the Ancient Greek oá¼°κονομῖα from oá¼¶κος (oikos, 'house') + vῐÓŒμος (nomos, 'custom' or 'law'), hence 'rules of the house(hold)'. Current _____ models developed out of the broader field of political economy in the late 19th century, owing to a desire to use an empirical approach more akin to the physical sciences.

a. Opportunity cost
b. Energy economics
c. Economic
d. Inflation

7. In microeconomics, _____ is quite simply the conversion of inputs into outputs. It is an economic process that uses resources to create a good or service that is suitable for exchange. This can include manufacturing, storing, shipping, and packaging.

a. Red Guards
b. Solved
c. Production
d. MET

Chapter 8. Competitive Firms and Markets

8. Economics:

    - _____, the desire to own something and the ability to pay for it
    - _____ curve, a graphic representation of a _____ schedule
    - _____ deposit, the money in checking accounts
    - _____ pull theory, the theory that inflation occurs when _____ for goods and services exceeds existing supplies
    - _____ schedule, a table that lists the quantity of a good a person will buy it each different price
    - _____ side economics, the school of economics at believes government spending and tax cuts open economy by raising _____

    a. Production
    b. Demand
    c. Variability
    d. McKesson ' Robbins scandal

9. In economics, the _____ can be defined as the graph depicting the relationship between the price of a certain commodity, and the amount of it that consumers are willing and able to purchase at that given price. It is a graphic representation of a demand schedule. The _____ for all consumers together follows from the _____ of every individual consumer: the individual demands at each price are added together.

    a. Wage curve
    b. Cost curve
    c. Kuznets curve
    d. Demand curve

10. _____ is a common market structure where many competing producers sell products that are differentiated from one another (ie. the products are substitutes, but are not exactly alike.) Many markets are monopolistically competitive, common examples include the markets for restaurants, cereal, clothing, shoes and service industries in large cities.

    a. Mathematical economics
    b. Perfect competition
    c. Monopolistic competition
    d. Financial crisis

11. _____ or economic opportunity loss is the value of the next best alternative foregone as the result of making a decision. _____ analysis is an important part of a company's decision-making processes but is not treated as an actual cost in any financial statement. The next best thing that a person can engage in is referred to as the _____ of doing the best thing and ignoring the next best thing to be done.

    a. Economic
    b. Industrial organization
    c. Economic ideology
    d. Opportunity cost

12. _____ in economics and business is the result of an exchange and from that trade we assign a numerical monetary value to a good, service or asset. If Alice trades Bob 4 apples for an orange, the _____ of an orange is 4 apples. Inversely, the _____ of an apple is 1/4 oranges.

    a. Price book
    b. Price war
    c. Price
    d. Premium pricing

Chapter 8. Competitive Firms and Markets

13. In economics and related disciplines, a _____ is a cost incurred in making an economic exchange. For example, most people, when buying or selling a stock, must pay a commission to their broker; that commission is a _____ of doing the stock deal. Or consider buying a banana from a store; to purchase the banana, your costs will be not only the price of the banana itself, but also the energy and effort it requires to find out which of the various banana products you prefer, where to get them and at what price, the cost of traveling from your house to the store and back, the time waiting in line, and the effort of the paying itself; the costs above and beyond the cost of the banana are the _____s.
   - a. Cost allocation
   - b. Cost of poor quality
   - c. Sliding scale fees
   - d. Transaction cost

14. _____ is an offer (often competitive) of setting a price one is willing to pay for something. A price offer is called a bid. The term may be used in context of auctions, stock exchange, card games, or real estate transactions.
   - a. Bord halfpenny
   - b. Central limit order book
   - c. Normal good
   - d. Bidding

15. A _____ is a counterfeit agreement among industries. It is an informal organization of producers that agree to coordinate prices and production. _____s usually occur in an oligopolistic industry, where there is a small number of sellers and usually involve homogeneous products.
   - a. Shill
   - b. Shanzhai
   - c. 100-year flood
   - d. Cartel

16. _____ is the transition of a national economy from monopoly control by groups of large businesses to a free market economy. This change rarely arises naturally, and is generally the result of regulation by a governing body.

    A modern example of _____ is the economic restructuring of Germany after the fall of the Third Reich in 1945.
   - a. Monopolization
   - b. Complementary monopoly
   - c. Decartelization
   - d. Market power

17. The _____ of a decision depends on both the cost of the alternative chosen and the benefit that the best alternative would have provided if chosen. _____ differs from accounting cost because it includes opportunity cost.
   - a. Isocost
   - b. Inventory analysis
   - c. Epstein-Zin preferences
   - d. Economic cost

18. An _____ is an easy accounted cost, such as wage, rent and materials. It can be transacted in the form of money payment and is lost directly, as opposed to monetary implicit costs.
   - a. Inventory valuation
   - b. Average variable cost
   - c. Explicit cost
   - d. Average fixed cost

19. In economics, an _____ occurs when one foregoes an alternative action but does not make an actual payment. (For instance, the explicit cost of a night at the movies includes the moviegoer's ticket and soda, but the _____ includes the pay he would have earned if he had chosen to work instead.) _____s are related to forgone benefits of any single transaction.
   - a. External sector
   - b. Ostrich strategy
   - c. Implicit cost
   - d. Overnight trade

20. In economics and business, specifically cost accounting, the _____ point (BEP) is the point at which cost or expenses and revenue are equal: there is no net loss or gain, and one has 'broken even'. A profit or a loss has not been made, although opportunity costs have been paid, and capital has received the risk-adjusted, expected return.

For example, if the business sells less than 200 tables each month, it will make a loss, if it sells more, it will be a profit.

   a. Nonmarket
   c. Buffer stock scheme

   b. Small numbers game
   d. Break-even

21. In microeconomics, _____ is the term used to refer to total when marginal cost is subtracted from marginal revenue. Under the marginal approach to profit maximization, to maximize profits, a firm should continue to produce a good until _____ is zero. Profit Maximization - The Marginal Approach.

   a. Corporate synergy
   c. Lehman scale

   b. Holding period return
   d. Marginal profit

Chapter 8. Competitive Firms and Markets

22. A _____ is:

- Rewrite _____, in generative grammar and computer science
- Standardization, a formal and widely-accepted statement, fact, definition, or qualification
- Operation, a determinate _____ for performing a mathematical operation and obtaining a certain result (Mathematics, Logic)
    - Unary operation
    - Binary operation
- _____ of inference, a function from sets of formulae to formulae (Mathematics, Logic)
- _____ of thumb, principle with broad application that is not intended to be strictly accurate or reliable for every situation. Also often simply referred to as a _____
- Moral, an atomic element of a moral code for guiding choices in human behavior
- Heuristic, a quantized '_____' which shows a tendency or probability for successful function
- A regulation, as in sports
- A Production _____, as in computer science
- Procedural law, a _____ set governing the application of laws to cases
    - A law, which may informally be called a '_____'
    - A court ruling, a decision by a court
- In the U.S. Government, a regulation mandated by Congress, but written or expanded upon by the Executive Branch.
- Norm (sociology), an informal but widely accepted _____, concept, truth, definition, or qualification (social norms, legal norms, coding norms)
- Norm (philosophy), a kind of sentence or a reason to act, feel or believe
- 'Rulership' is the concept of governance by a government:
    - Military _____, governance by a military body
    - Monastic _____, a collection of precepts that guides the life of monks or nuns in a religious order where the superior holds the place of Christ
- Slide _____

- '_____,' a song by Ayumi Hamasaki
- '_____,' a song by rapper Nas
- '_____s,' an album by the band The Whitest Boy Alive
- _____s: Pyaar Ka Superhit Formula, a 2003 Bollywood film
- ruler, an instrument for measuring lengths
- _____, a component of an astrolabe, circumferator or similar instrument
- The _____s, a bestselling self-help book
- _____ Project (Run Up-to-date Linux Everywhere), a project that aims to use up-to-date Linux software on old PCs
- _____ engine, a software system that helps managing business _____s
- Ja _____, a hip hop artist
    - R.U.L.E., a 2005 greatest hits album by rapper Ja _____
- '_____s,' a KMFDM song

a. Demand
b. Procter ' Gamble
c. Rule
d. Technocracy

Chapter 8. Competitive Firms and Markets

23. In economics and finance, _____ is the change in total cost that arises when the quantity produced changes by one unit. It is the cost of producing one more unit of a good. Mathematically, the _____ function is expressed as the first derivative of the total cost (TC) function with respect to quantity (Q.)
    a. Khozraschyot
    b. Quality costs
    c. Marginal cost
    d. Variable cost

24. In microeconomics, _____ is the extra revenue that an additional unit of product will bring. It is the additional income from selling one more unit of a good; sometimes equal to price. It can also be described as the change in total revenue/change in number of units sold.
    a. Reservation price
    b. Long term
    c. Marginal revenue
    d. Market demand schedule

25. In economics and business decision-making, _____ are costs that cannot be recovered once they have been incurred. _____ are sometimes contrasted with variable costs, which are the costs that will change due to the proposed course of action, and prospective costs which are costs that will be incurred if an action is taken.

In traditional microeconomic theory, only variable costs are relevant to a decision.

    a. Hyperbolic discounting
    b. Sunk costs
    c. Halo effect
    d. Post-purchase rationalization

26. In economics, the concept of the _____ refers to the decision-making time frame of a firm in which at least one factor of production is fixed. Costs which are fixed in the _____ have no impact on a firms decisions. For example a firm can raise output by increasing the amount of labour through overtime.
    a. Product Pipeline
    b. Hicks-neutral technical change
    c. Productivity model
    d. Short-run

27. _____ are the estimated quantities of crude oil that are claimed to be recoverable under existing economic and operating conditions.

The total estimated amount of oil in an oil reservoir, including both producible and non-producible oil, is called oil in place. However, because of reservoir characteristics and limitations in petroleum extraction technologies only a fraction of this oil can be brought to the surface, and it is only this producible fraction that is considered to be reserves.

    a. Oil reserves in the United States
    b. Oil depletion
    c. Oil reserves
    d. Olduvai theory

28. _____ are the prices that the factors of production of a finished item attract.

There has been some economic debate as to what determines these prices. Classical and Marxist economists argued that the _____ decided the value of a product and so value was intrinsic within the product.

    a. Factor prices
    b. Marginal product
    c. Productivity model
    d. Marginal product of labor

29. In economic models, the _____ time frame assumes no fixed factors of production. Firms can enter or leave the marketplace, and the cost (and availability) of land, labor, raw materials, and capital goods can be assumed to vary. In contrast, in the short-run time frame, certain factors are assumed to be fixed, because there is not sufficient time for them to change.

   a. Productivity world
   b. Long-run
   c. Price/performance ratio
   d. Diseconomies of scale

30. Competitive market equilibrium is the traditional concept of economic equilibrium, appropriate for the analysis of commodity markets with flexible prices and many traders, and serving as the benchmark of efficiency in economic analysis. It relies crucially on the assumption of a competitive environment where each trader decides upon a quantity that is so small compared to the total quantity traded in the market that their individual transactions have no influence on the prices. Competitive markets are an ideal, a standard that other market structures are evaluated by.

A _____ consists of a vector of prices and an allocation such that given the prices, each trader by maximizing his objective function (profit, preferences) subject to his technological possibilities and resource constraints plans to trade into his part of the proposed allocation, and such that the prices make all net trades compatible with one another ('clear the market') by equating aggregate supply and demand for the commodities which are traded.

   a. Product-Market Growth Matrix
   b. Competitive equilibrium
   c. Partial equilibrium
   d. Market system

31. _____ is a term used by economists to describe a condition in which firms can freely enter the market for an economic good by establishing production and beginning to sell the product.

_____ is implied by the perfect competition condition that there is an unlimited number of buyers and sellers in a market. In comparison to perfect competition, however, _____ is a condition often more applicable to real world conditions.

   a. 130-30 fund
   b. 100-year flood
   c. 1921 recession
   d. Free entry

32. _____ is the production of large amounts of standardized products, including and especially on assembly lines. The concepts of _____ are applied to various kinds of products, from fluids and particulates handled in bulk to discrete solid parts to assemblies of such parts

_____ of assemblies typically uses electric-motor-powered moving tracks or conveyor belts to move partially complete products to workers, who perform simple repetitive tasks.

   a. 130-30 fund
   b. 100-year flood
   c. 1921 recession
   d. Mass production

33. _____ is a Financial term that refers to the revenue or cost to be expected in the following fiscal period as a derivative of the performance in the current period.

Chapter 8. Competitive Firms and Markets

When used in the context of revenue, _____ refers to the income expected in the following period as a result of sales closed in the existing period (assuming no further sales are made.) If a company worked throughout the year and managed to signed up deals that will generate 1M USD a year in the following year (assuming no additional sales), then it would be said that company has 1M USD _____ in this year.

a. Exit rate
b. Offshore financial centre
c. Unsecured creditor
d. Asset-liability mismatch

34. In economics, _____ is when quantity supplied is more than quantity demanded. .
a. Excess supply
b. Effective unemployment rate
c. Economic Value Creation
d. Illicit financial flows

35. In economics, _____ is the ratio of the percent change in one variable to the percent change in another variable. It is a tool for measuring the responsiveness of a function to changes in parameters in a relative way. Commonly analyzed are _____ of substitution, price and wealth.
a. ACCRA Cost of Living Index
b. ACEA agreement
c. Elasticity
d. Elasticity of demand

36. In economics, economic equilibrium is simply a state of the world where economic forces are balanced and in the absence of external influences the (equilibrium) values of economic variables will not change. It is the point at which quantity demanded and quantity supplied are equal. _____, for example, refers to a condition where a market price is established through competition such that the amount of goods or services sought by buyers is equal to the amount of goods or services produced by sellers.
a. Product-Market Growth Matrix
b. Regulated market
c. Marketization
d. Market equilibrium

37. An _____ is a tax based on the value of real estate or personal property. It is more common than the opposite, a specific duty, or a tax based on the quantity of an item regardless of price.

An _____ is typically imposed at the time of a transaction), but it may be imposed on an annual basis (real or personal property tax) or in connection with another significant event (inheritance tax, surrendering citizenship, or tariffs.)

a. Indirect tax
b. User charge
c. Ad valorem tax
d. Optimal tax

38. _____ is a tax charged by some US states to corporations formed in those states based on the number of shares they issue or, in some cases, the amount of their assets. The purpose of the tax is to raise revenue for the state. The State of Delaware has a significant _____, while other states, such as Nevada, have none at all or a smaller one.
a. Current use
b. Tax policy
c. Tax reform
d. Franchise tax

39. A _____ is a consumption tax charged at the point of purchase for certain goods and services. The tax is usually set as a percentage by the government charging the tax. There is usually a list of exemptions.

Chapter 8. Competitive Firms and Markets

a. 130-30 fund
b. 1921 recession
c. Sales tax
d. 100-year flood

40. A _____ is a duty imposed on goods when they are moved across a political boundary. They are usually associated with protectionism, the economic policy of restraining trade between nations. For political reasons, _____s are usually imposed on imported goods, although they may also be imposed on exported goods.

a. 100-year flood
b. 1921 recession
c. Tariff
d. 130-30 fund

41. To _____ is to impose a financial charge or other levy upon a taxpayer by a state or the functional equivalent of a state.

_____es are also imposed by many subnational entities. _____es consist of direct _____ or indirect _____, and may be paid in money or as its labour equivalent (often but not always unpaid.)

a. Tax
b. 1921 recession
c. 130-30 fund
d. 100-year flood

42. A _____ refers to property being sold by a taxing authority or the court to recover delinquent taxes.

When property taxes are not paid, title gets transferred to the state. The owner will then have a period of time to redeem the property by paying the overdue taxes, including penalties and costs.

a. Tax competition
b. Taxation as theft
c. Tax Sale
d. Tax wedge

43. To tax is to impose a financial charge or other levy upon a taxpayer by a state or the functional equivalent of a state.

_____ are also imposed by many subnational entities. _____ consist of direct tax or indirect tax, and may be paid in money or as its labour equivalent (often but not always unpaid.)

a. 130-30 fund
b. 100-year flood
c. Taxes
d. 1921 recession

44. Economic _____ is defined as an excess distribution to any factor in a production process above that which is required to induce the factor into the process or any excess above that which is necessary to keep the factor in its current use..

Classical Factor _____ is primarily concerned with the fee paid for the use of fixed (e.g. natural) resources. The classical definition is expressed as any excess payment above that required to induce or provide for production.

a. 1921 recession
b. Rent
c. 100-year flood
d. 130-30 fund

Chapter 9. Applying the Competitive Model

1. _____ is a broad label that refers to any individuals or households that use goods and services generated within the economy. The concept of a _____ is used in different contexts, so that the usage and significance of the term may vary.

Typically when business people and economists talk of _____ s they are talking about person as _____, an aggregated commodity item with little individuality other than that expressed in the buy/not-buy decision.

 a. 130-30 fund
 b. 100-year flood
 c. 1921 recession
 d. Consumer

2. The Court of Justice of the European Communities, usually called the _____, is the highest court in the European Union in matters of European Community law. It has the ultimate say on matters of EU law in order to ensure its equal application across all EU member states.

The court was established in 1952 and is -- unlike most other Union institutions -- based in Luxembourg.

 a. European Court of Justice
 b. European Union
 c. ACEA agreement
 d. ACCRA Cost of Living Index

3. The _____ is an economic and political union of 27 member states, located primarily in Europe. It was established by the Treaty of Maastricht on 1 November 1993, upon the foundations of the pre-existing European Economic Community. With a population of almost 500 million, the _____ generates an estimated 30% share (US$18.4 trillion in 2008) of the nominal gross world product.

 a. European Union
 b. ACCRA Cost of Living Index
 c. ACEA agreement
 d. European Court of Justice

4. An _____ is a tax levied on the financial income of people, corporations, or other legal entities. Various _____ systems exist, with varying degrees of tax incidence. Income taxation can be progressive, proportional, or regressive.

 a. ACCRA Cost of Living Index
 b. AD-IA Model
 c. ACEA agreement
 d. Income tax

5. A _____ is a consumption tax charged at the point of purchase for certain goods and services. The tax is usually set as a percentage by the government charging the tax. There is usually a list of exemptions.

 a. 100-year flood
 b. 1921 recession
 c. Sales tax
 d. 130-30 fund

6. To _____ is to impose a financial charge or other levy upon a taxpayer by a state or the functional equivalent of a state.

_____ es are also imposed by many subnational entities. _____ es consist of direct _____ or indirect _____, and may be paid in money or as its labour equivalent (often but not always unpaid.)

 a. 100-year flood
 b. 130-30 fund
 c. Tax
 d. 1921 recession

7. To tax is to impose a financial charge or other levy upon a taxpayer by a state or the functional equivalent of a state.

_____ are also imposed by many subnational entities. _____ consist of direct tax or indirect tax, and may be paid in money or as its labour equivalent (often but not always unpaid.)

- a. 1921 recession
- b. Taxes
- c. 130-30 fund
- d. 100-year flood

8. A _____ is a price discrimination technique in which the price of a product or service is composed of two parts - a lump-sum fee as well as a per-unit charge. In general, price discrimination techniques only occur in partially or fully monopolistic markets. It is designed to enable the firm to capture more consumer surplus than it otherwise would in a non-discriminating pricing environment.

- a. Two-part tariff
- b. Penetration pricing
- c. Price floor
- d. Big ticket item

9. _____ is a branch of economics that uses microeconomic techniques to simultaneously determine allocative efficiency within an economy and the income distribution associated with it. It analyzes social welfare, however measured, in terms of economic activities of the individuals that comprise the theoretical society considered. As such, individuals, with associated economic activities, are the basic units for aggregating to social welfare, whether of a group, a community, or a society, and there is no 'social welfare' apart from the 'welfare' associated with its individual units.

- a. General equilibrium
- b. Tobit model
- c. Law of increasing costs
- d. Welfare economics

10. The _____ is an important selective, mainly private, international organization designed by its founders to supervise and liberalize international trade. The organization officially commenced on 1 January 1995, under the Marrakesh Agreement, succeeding the 1947 General Agreement on Tariffs and Trade (GATT.)

The _____ deals with regulation of trade between participating countries; it provides a framework for negotiating and formalising trade agreements, and a dispute resolution process aimed at enforcing participants' adherence to _____ agreements which are signed by representatives of member governments and ratified by their parliaments.

- a. World Trade Organization
- b. Backus-Kehoe-Kydland consumption correlation puzzle
- c. 2009 G-20 London summit protests
- d. Bio-energy village

11. In economics, a common-pool resource, alternatively termed a _____ resource, is a particular type of good consisting of a natural or human-made resource system, the size or characteristics of which makes it costly, but not impossible, to exclude potential beneficiaries from obtaining benefits from its use. Unlike pure public goods, common pool resources face problems of congestion or overuse, because they are subtractable. A common-pool resource typically consists of a core resource, which defines the stock variable, while providing a limited quantity of extractable fringe units, which defines the flow variable.

- a. Common-pool resource
- b. Government monopoly
- c. Price-cap regulation
- d. Common property

Chapter 9. Applying the Competitive Model

12. Economics:

    - _____, the desire to own something and the ability to pay for it
    - _____ curve, a graphic representation of a _____ schedule
    - _____ deposit, the money in checking accounts
    - _____ pull theory, the theory that inflation occurs when _____ for goods and services exceeds existing supplies
    - _____ schedule, a table that lists the quantity of a good a person will buy it each different price
    - _____ side economics, the school of economics at believes government spending and tax cuts open economy by raising _____

    a. Production
    b. McKesson ' Robbins scandal
    c. Variability
    d. Demand

13. In economics, the _____ can be defined as the graph depicting the relationship between the price of a certain commodity, and the amount of it that consumers are willing and able to purchase at that given price. It is a graphic representation of a demand schedule. The _____ for all consumers together follows from the _____ of every individual consumer: the individual demands at each price are added together.

    a. Kuznets curve
    b. Cost curve
    c. Wage curve
    d. Demand curve

14. _____s is the social science that studies the production, distribution, and consumption of goods and services. The term _____s comes from the Ancient Greek oá¼°κονομῖα from oá¼¶κος (oikos, 'house') + vΐŒμος (nomos, 'custom' or 'law'), hence 'rules of the house(hold)'. Current _____ models developed out of the broader field of political economy in the late 19th century, owing to a desire to use an empirical approach more akin to the physical sciences.

    a. Energy economics
    b. Opportunity cost
    c. Inflation
    d. Economic

15. In economics, an _____ is any good or commodity, transported from one country to another country in a legitimate fashion, typically for use in trade. _____ goods or services are provided to foreign consumers by domestic producers. _____ is an important part of international trade.

    a. ACCRA Cost of Living Index
    b. Export
    c. AD-IA Model
    d. ACEA agreement

16. _____ is an economic model based on price, utility and quantity in a market. It predicts that in a competitive market, price will function to equalize the quantity demanded by consumers, and the quantity supplied by producers, resulting in an economic equilibrium of price and quantity. The model incorporates other factors changing equilibrium as a shift of demand and/or supply.

    a. Joint demand
    b. Supply and demand
    c. Rational addiction
    d. Deferred gratification

17. A _____ is a duty imposed on goods when they are moved across a political boundary. They are usually associated with protectionism, the economic policy of restraining trade between nations. For political reasons, _____s are usually imposed on imported goods, although they may also be imposed on exported goods.

Chapter 9. Applying the Competitive Model

a. 1921 recession
b. 130-30 fund
c. 100-year flood
d. Tariff

18. A _____ is an object whose consumption increases the utility of the consumer, for which the quantity demanded exceeds the quantity supplied at zero price. _____s are usually modeled as having diminishing marginal utility. The first individual purchase has high utility; the second has less.
   a. Good
   b. Pie method
   c. Merit good
   d. Composite good

19. In economics, _____ is a measure of the relative satisfaction from consumption of various goods and services. Given this measure, one may speak meaningfully of increasing or decreasing _____, and thereby explain economic behavior in terms of attempts to increase one's _____. For illustrative purposes, changes in _____ are sometimes expressed in units called utils.
   a. Ordinal utility
   b. Utility
   c. Utility function
   d. Expected utility hypothesis

20. While preferences are the conventional foundation of microeconomics, it is often convenient to represent preferences with a _____ and reason indirectly about preferences with _____s. Let X be the consumption set, the set of all mutually-exclusive packages the consumer could conceivably consume (such as an indifference curve map without the indifference curves.) The consumer's _____ $u: X \to \mathbf{R}$ ranks each package in the consumption set.
   a. Utility function
   b. Expected utility hypothesis
   c. Utility
   d. Ordinal utility

21. _____ is the a method of technical and economic research of the systems for purpose to optimize a parity between system's consumer functions or properties and expenses to achieve those functions or properties.

This methodology for continuous perfection of production, industrial technologies, organizational structures was developed by Juryj Sobolev in 1948 at the 'Perm telephone factory'

- 1948 Juryj Sobolev - the first success in application of a method analysis at the 'Perm telephone factory' .
- 1949 - the first application for the invention as result of use of the new method.

Today in economically developed countries practically each enterprise or the company use methodology of the kind of functional-cost analysis as a practice of the quality management, most full satisfying to principles of standards of series ISO 9000.

- Interest of consumer not in products itself, but the advantage which it will receive from its usage.
- The consumer aspires to reduce his expenses
- Functions needed by consumer can be executed in the various ways, and, hence, with various efficiency and expenses. Among possible alternatives of realization of functions exist such in which the parity of quality and the price is the optimal for the consumer.

The goal of _____ is achievement of the highest consumer satisfaction of production at simultaneous decrease in all kinds of industrial expenses Classical _____ has three English synonyms - Value Engineering, Value Management, Value Analysis.

Chapter 9. Applying the Competitive Model

a. Monopoly wage
c. Function cost analysis
b. Willingness to pay
d. Staple financing

22. In economics, the _____ is the maximum amount a person would be willing to pay, sacrifice or exchange for a good.

Choice modelling techniques may be used to estimate the value of the _____ through a choice experiment.

a. Global strategy
c. Round-tripping
b. Net pay
d. Willingness to pay

23. The term surplus is used in economics for several related quantities. The _____ is the amount that consumers benefit by being able to purchase a product for a price that is less than they would be willing to pay. The producer surplus is the amount that producers benefit by selling at a market price mechanism that is higher than they would be willing to sell for.

a. Marginal rate of technical substitution
c. Microeconomic reform
b. Necessity good
d. Consumer surplus

24. _____ is a specific term used in companies' financial reporting from the company-whole point of view. Because that use excludes the effects of changing ownership interest, an economic measure of _____ is necessary for financial analysis from the shareholders' point of view

_____ is defined by the Financial Accounting Standards Board, or FASB, as e;the change in equity [net assets] of a business enterprise during a period from transactions and other events and circumstances from nonowner sources. It includes all changes in equity during a period except those resulting from investments by owners and distributions to owners.e;

_____ is the sum of net income and other items that must bypass the income statement because they have not been realized, including items like an unrealized holding gain or loss from available for sale securities and foreign currency translation gains or losses.

a. Real income
c. Windfall gain
b. Net national income
d. Comprehensive income

25. _____ in economics and business is the result of an exchange and from that trade we assign a numerical monetary value to a good, service or asset. If Alice trades Bob 4 apples for an orange, the _____ of an orange is 4 apples. Inversely, the _____ of an apple is 1/4 oranges.

a. Price book
c. Premium pricing
b. Price war
d. Price

26. In economics and finance, _____ is the change in total cost that arises when the quantity produced changes by one unit. It is the cost of producing one more unit of a good. Mathematically, the _____ function is expressed as the first derivative of the total cost (TC) function with respect to quantity (Q.)

a. Quality costs
c. Khozraschyot
b. Variable cost
d. Marginal cost

27. The term surplus is used in economics for several related quantities. The consumer surplus is the amount that consumers benefit by being able to purchase a product for a price that is less than they would be willing to pay. The _____ is the amount that producers benefit by selling at a market price mechanism that is higher than they would be willing to sell for.
   a. Long term
   b. Schedule delay
   c. Returns to scale
   d. Producer surplus

28. In economics, a _____ is a graph of the costs of production as a function of total quantity produced. In a free market economy, productively efficient firms use these curves to find the optimal point of production, where they make the most profits. There are a few different types of _____s, each relevant to a different area of economics.
   a. Demand curve
   b. Phillips curve
   c. Kuznets curve
   d. Cost curve

29. _____ is a common market structure where many competing producers sell products that are differentiated from one another (ie. the products are substitutes, but are not exactly alike.) Many markets are monopolistically competitive, common examples include the markets for restaurants, cereal, clothing, shoes and service industries in large cities.
   a. Perfect competition
   b. Financial crisis
   c. Monopolistic competition
   d. Mathematical economics

30. A _____ is a counterfeit agreement among industries. It is an informal organization of producers that agree to coordinate prices and production. _____s usually occur in an oligopolistic industry, where there is a small number of sellers and usually involve homogeneous products.
   a. Shanzhai
   b. Shill
   c. 100-year flood
   d. Cartel

31. _____ is the transition of a national economy from monopoly control by groups of large businesses to a free market economy. This change rarely arises naturally, and is generally the result of regulation by a governing body.

A modern example of _____ is the economic restructuring of Germany after the fall of the Third Reich in 1945.

   a. Monopolization
   b. Complementary monopoly
   c. Decartelization
   d. Market power

32. In economics, a _____ is a loss of economic efficiency that can occur when equilibrium for a good or service is not Pareto optimal. In other words, either people who would have more marginal benefit than marginal cost are not buying the good or service, or people who would have more marginal cost than marginal benefit are buying the product.

Causes of _____ can include monopoly pricing, externalities, taxes or subsidies, and binding price ceilings or floors.

   a. Leapfrogging
   b. Deadweight loss
   c. Contract curve
   d. Distributive efficiency

33. In economics, a _____ exists when the production or use of goods and services by the market is not efficient. That is, there exists another outcome where all involved can be made better off. _____s can be viewed as scenarios where individuals' pursuit of pure self-interest leads to results that are not efficient - that can be improved upon from the societal point-of-view.
   a. Fixed exchange rate
   b. Market failure
   c. General equilibrium
   d. Financial economics

34. Necessary _____s:

If x is a necessary _____ of y, then the presence of y necessarily implies the presence of x. The presence of x, however, does not imply that y will occur.

Sufficient _____s:

If x is a sufficient _____ of y, then the presence of x necessarily implies the presence of y.

   a. Cause
   b. Philosophy of economics
   c. Materialism
   d. Political philosophy

35. Competitive market equilibrium is the traditional concept of economic equilibrium, appropriate for the analysis of commodity markets with flexible prices and many traders, and serving as the benchmark of efficiency in economic analysis. It relies crucially on the assumption of a competitive environment where each trader decides upon a quantity that is so small compared to the total quantity traded in the market that their individual transactions have no influence on the prices.Competitive markets are an ideal, a standard that other market structures are evaluated by.

A _____ consists of a vector of prices and an allocation such that given the prices, each trader by maximizing his objective function (profit, preferences) subject to his technological possibilities and resource constraints plans to trade into his part of the proposed allocation, and such that the prices make all net trades compatible with one another ('clear the market') by equating aggregate supply and demand for the commodities which are traded.

   a. Partial equilibrium
   b. Market system
   c. Product-Market Growth Matrix
   d. Competitive equilibrium

36. Economic _____ is defined as an excess distribution to any factor in a production process above that which is required to induce the factor into the process or any excess above that which is necessary to keep the factor in its current use..

Classical Factor _____ is primarily concerned with the fee paid for the use of fixed (e.g. natural) resources. The classical definition is expressed as any excess payment above that required to induce or provide for production.

   a. 1921 recession
   b. Rent
   c. 100-year flood
   d. 130-30 fund

37. In economics, _____ are business expenses that are not dependent on the activities of the business They tend to be time-related, such as salaries or rents being paid per month. This is in contrast to variable costs, which are volume-related (and are paid per quantity.)

In management accounting, _____ are defined as expenses that do not change in proportion to the activity of a business, within the relevant period or scale of production.

   a. Fixed costs
   c. Quality costs
   b. Cost-Volume-Profit Analysis
   d. Cost of poor quality

38. _____ or economic opportunity loss is the value of the next best alternative foregone as the result of making a decision. _____ analysis is an important part of a company's decision-making processes but is not treated as an actual cost in any financial statement. The next best thing that a person can engage in is referred to as the _____ of doing the best thing and ignoring the next best thing to be done.

   a. Industrial organization
   c. Economic ideology
   b. Opportunity cost
   d. Economic

39. _____ are the income that is gained by governments because of taxation of the people.

Just as there are different types of tax, the form in which _____ is collected also differs; furthermore, the agency that collects the tax may not be part of central government, but may be an alternative third-party licenced to collect tax which they themselves will use. For example:

  • In the UK, the DVLA collects road tax, which is then passed on the treasury.

_____s on purchases can come from two forms: 'tax' itself is a percentage of the price added to the purchase (such as sales tax in US states, or VAT in the UK), while 'duty' is a fixed amount added to the purchase price (such as is commonly found on cigarettes.) In order to calculate the total tax raised from these sales, we must work out the effective tax rate multiplied by the quantity supplied.

   a. Tax revenue
   c. Tax and spend
   b. Taxation as slavery
   d. Taxable wage

40. An _____ is a tax based on the value of real estate or personal property. It is more common than the opposite, a specific duty, or a tax based on the quantity of an item regardless of price.

An _____ is typically imposed at the time of a transaction), but it may be imposed on an annual basis (real or personal property tax) or in connection with another significant event (inheritance tax, surrendering citizenship, or tariffs.)

   a. Optimal tax
   c. Indirect tax
   b. User charge
   d. Ad valorem tax

41. A _____ refers to property being sold by a taxing authority or the court to recover delinquent taxes.

Chapter 9. Applying the Competitive Model
69

When property taxes are not paid, title gets transferred to the state. The owner will then have a period of time to redeem the property by paying the overdue taxes, including penalties and costs.

a. Taxation as theft
b. Tax wedge
c. Tax competition
d. Tax Sale

42. A _____ is a government- or group-imposed limit on how low a price can be charged for a product. In order for a _____ to be effective, it must be greater than the equilibrium price. An ineffective _____, below equilibrium price.

A _____ can be set below the free-market equilibrium price.

a. Price markdown
b. Flat rate
c. Two-part tariff
d. Price floor

43. In economics, a _____ may be either a subsidy or a price control, both with the intended effect of keeping the market price of a good higher than the competitive equilibrium level.

In the case of a price control, a _____ is the minimum legal price a seller may charge, typically placed above equilibrium. It is the support of certain price levels at or above market values by the government.

a. Marginal profit
b. Labor intensity
c. Payment schedule
d. Price support

44. _____ is a common concept in economics, and gives rise to derived concepts such as consumer debt. Generally _____ is defined by opposition to production. But the precise definition can vary because different schools of economists define production quite differently.

a. Cash or share options
b. Foreclosure data providers
c. Federal Reserve Bank Notes
d. Consumption

45. A _____ is the transfer of wealth from one party (such as a person or company) to another. A _____ is usually made in exchange for the provision of goods, services or both, or to fulfill a legal obligation.

The simplest and oldest form of _____ is barter, the exchange of one good or service for another.

a. Soft count
b. Social gravity
c. Going concern
d. Payment

46. A _____ is a government imposed limit on how high a price can be charged on a product. For a _____ to be effective, it must differ from the free market price. In the graph at right, the supply and demand curves intersect to determine the free-market quantity and price.

a. Price ceiling
b. Product sabotage
c. Fire sale
d. Pricing

Chapter 9. Applying the Competitive Model

47. In economics, _____ is the ratio of the percent change in one variable to the percent change in another variable. It is a tool for measuring the responsiveness of a function to changes in parameters in a relative way. Commonly analyzed are _____ of substitution, price and wealth.
   a. Elasticity
   b. ACCRA Cost of Living Index
   c. Elasticity of demand
   d. ACEA agreement

48. _____ is a type of trade policy that allows traders to act and transact without interference from government. Thus, the policy permits trading partners mutual gains from trade, with goods and services produced according to the theory of comparative advantage.

   Under a _____ policy, prices are a reflection of true supply and demand, and are the sole determinant of resource allocation.

   a. Free trade
   b. 1921 recession
   c. 100-year flood
   d. 130-30 fund

49. In economics, an _____ is any good (e.g. a commodity) or service brought into one country from another country in a legitimate fashion, typically for use in trade. It is a good that is brought in from another country for sale. _____ goods or services are provided to domestic consumers by foreign producers. An _____ in the receiving country is an export to the sending country.
   a. Economic integration
   b. Import quota
   c. Incoterms
   d. Import

50. In economics, _____ occurs when an individual, organization or firm seeks to make money through economic rent.

   _____ generally implies the extraction of uncompensated value from others without making any contribution to productivity, such as by gaining control of land and other pre-existing natural resources, or by imposing burdensome regulations or other government decisions that may affect consumers or businesses. While there may be few people in modern industrialized countries who do not gain something, directly or indirectly, through some form or another of _____, Rent seeking in the aggregate imposes substantial losses on society.

   a. 130-30 fund
   b. 100-year flood
   c. Good governance
   d. Rent seeking

Chapter 10. General Equilibrium and Economic Welfare

1. _____, 1st Baron Keynes was a renowned economist from Britain whose many ideas on economic and political theories as well as on many governments' monetary policies influenced America. He advocated a government that played an active role in the lives of people regarding business, economy, etc. In this role, the government would use fiscal measures to reduce the consequences of recessions, economic depressions and booms.
   a. John Maynard Keynes
   b. Adam Smith
   c. Adolf Hitler
   d. Adolph Fischer

2. The _____ states that, for many events, roughly 80% of the effects come from 20% of the causes. Business management thinker Joseph M. Juran suggested the principle and named it after Italian economist Vilfredo Pareto, who observed that 80% of the land in Italy was owned by 20% of the population. It is a common rule of thumb in business; e.g., '80% of your sales come from 20% of your clients.' Mathematically, where something is shared among a sufficiently large set of participants, there will always be a number k between 50 and 100 such that k% is taken by% of the participants.
   a. Competition law
   b. Pareto principle
   c. Minimum wage law
   d. Beneficial ownership

3. Competitive market equilibrium is the traditional concept of economic equilibrium, appropriate for the analysis of commodity markets with flexible prices and many traders, and serving as the benchmark of efficiency in economic analysis. It relies crucially on the assumption of a competitive environment where each trader decides upon a quantity that is so small compared to the total quantity traded in the market that their individual transactions have no influence on the prices. Competitive markets are an ideal, a standard that other market structures are evaluated by.

   A _____ consists of a vector of prices and an allocation such that given the prices, each trader by maximizing his objective function (profit, preferences) subject to his technological possibilities and resource constraints plans to trade into his part of the proposed allocation, and such that the prices make all net trades compatible with one another ('clear the market') by equating aggregate supply and demand for the commodities which are traded.

   a. Product-Market Growth Matrix
   b. Competitive equilibrium
   c. Market system
   d. Partial equilibrium

4. _____s is the social science that studies the production, distribution, and consumption of goods and services. The term _____s comes from the Ancient Greek oá¼°κονομῖα from oá¼¶κος (oikos, 'house') + vÏŒμος (nomos, 'custom' or 'law'), hence 'rules of the house(hold)'. Current _____ models developed out of the broader field of political economy in the late 19th century, owing to a desire to use an empirical approach more akin to the physical sciences.
   a. Opportunity cost
   b. Inflation
   c. Energy economics
   d. Economic

5. _____ is the concept or idea of fairness in economics, particularly as to taxation or welfare economics.

   In welfare economics, _____ may be distinguished from economic efficiency in overall evaluation of social welfare. Although '_____' has broader uses, it may be posed as a counterpart to economic inequality in yielding a 'good' distribution of welfare.

   a. ACCRA Cost of Living Index
   b. ACEA agreement
   c. AD-IA Model
   d. Equity

Chapter 10. General Equilibrium and Economic Welfare

6. _____ theory is a branch of theoretical economics. It seeks to explain the behavior of supply, demand and prices in a whole economy with several or many markets. It is often assumed that agents are price takers and in that setting two common notions of equilibrium exist: Walrasian (or competitive) equilibrium, and its generalization; a price equilibrium with transfers.
   - a. Human capital
   - b. Rational choice theory
   - c. New Keynesian economics
   - d. General equilibrium

7. In economics, economic equilibrium is simply a state of the world where economic forces are balanced and in the absence of external influences the (equilibrium) values of economic variables will not change. It is the point at which quantity demanded and quantity supplied are equal. _____, for example, refers to a condition where a market price is established through competition such that the amount of goods or services sought by buyers is equal to the amount of goods or services produced by sellers.
   - a. Regulated market
   - b. Marketization
   - c. Product-Market Growth Matrix
   - d. Market equilibrium

8. In microeconomics, _____ is quite simply the conversion of inputs into outputs. It is an economic process that uses resources to create a good or service that is suitable for exchange. This can include manufacturing, storing, shipping, and packaging.
   - a. Solved
   - b. Red Guards
   - c. MET
   - d. Production

9. _____ is a term used to described a tendency or preference towards a particular perspective, ideology or result, especially when the tendency interferes with the ability to be impartial, unprejudiced, or objective. The term _____ed is used to describe an action, judgment, or other outcome influenced by a prejudged perspective. It is also used to refer to a person or body of people whose actions or judgments exhibit _____.
   - a. 100-year flood
   - b. Bias
   - c. 1921 recession
   - d. 130-30 fund

10. _____s are externalities of economic activity or processes upon those who are not directly involved in it. Odours from a rendering plant are negative _____s upon its neighbours; the beauty of a homeowner's flower garden is a positive _____ upon neighbours.

In the same way, the economic benefits of increased trade are the _____s anticipated in the formation of multilateral alliances of many of the regional nation states: e.g. SARC (South Asian Regional Cooperation), ASpillover effectAN (Association of South East Asian Nations)

In reference to psychology, the _____ is when other people's emotions affect the emotions of those around them.

   - a. Business sector
   - b. Cobb-Douglas
   - c. Public good
   - d. Spillover effect

11. A _____ is a counterfeit agreement among industries. It is an informal organization of producers that agree to coordinate prices and production. _____s usually occur in an oligopolistic industry, where there is a small number of sellers and usually involve homogeneous products.

a. Shanzhai
c. Shill
b. 100-year flood
d. Cartel

12. _____ is the transition of a national economy from monopoly control by groups of large businesses to a free market economy. This change rarely arises naturally, and is generally the result of regulation by a governing body.

A modern example of _____ is the economic restructuring of Germany after the fall of the Third Reich in 1945.

a. Decartelization
c. Monopolization
b. Market power
d. Complementary monopoly

13. A _____ is the lowest hourly, daily or monthly wage that employers may legally pay to employees or workers. Equivalently, it is the lowest wage at which workers may sell their labor. Although _____ laws are in effect in a great many jurisdictions, there are differences of opinion about the benefits and drawbacks of a _____.

a. Permanent war economy
c. Microfoundations
b. Minimum wage
d. Marginal propensity to consume

14. _____ is the body of law which prohibits employers from hiring employees or workers for less than a given hourly, daily or monthly minimum wage. More than 90% of all countries have some kind of minimum wage legislation.

Until relatively recently, _____s were usually very tightly focused.

a. Home country control
c. Bankruptcy in Canada
b. Minimum wage law
d. Joint venture

15. An _____ is a tax based on the value of real estate or personal property. It is more common than the opposite, a specific duty, or a tax based on the quantity of an item regardless of price.

An _____ is typically imposed at the time of a transaction), but it may be imposed on an annual basis (real or personal property tax) or in connection with another significant event (inheritance tax, surrendering citizenship, or tariffs.)

a. Indirect tax
c. Optimal tax
b. User charge
d. Ad valorem tax

16. In economics, an _____ is a way of representing various distributions of resources. Edgeworth made his presentation in his famous book, Mathematical Psychics: An essay on the application of mathematics to the moral sciences, 1881. Edgeworth's original two axis depiction was developed into the now familiar box diagram by Pareto in 1906 and was popularized in a later exposition by Bowley.

a. Equivalent variation
c. International Social Security Association
b. ACCRA Cost of Living Index
d. Edgeworth box

17. A _____ is a consumption tax charged at the point of purchase for certain goods and services. The tax is usually set as a percentage by the government charging the tax. There is usually a list of exemptions.

Chapter 10. General Equilibrium and Economic Welfare

   a. 1921 recession
   b. 100-year flood
   c. 130-30 fund
   d. Sales tax

18. A _____ is a duty imposed on goods when they are moved across a political boundary. They are usually associated with protectionism, the economic policy of restraining trade between nations. For political reasons, _____s are usually imposed on imported goods, although they may also be imposed on exported goods.
   a. 130-30 fund
   b. 1921 recession
   c. 100-year flood
   d. Tariff

19. To _____ is to impose a financial charge or other levy upon a taxpayer by a state or the functional equivalent of a state.

   _____es are also imposed by many subnational entities. _____es consist of direct _____ or indirect _____, and may be paid in money or as its labour equivalent (often but not always unpaid.)

   a. Tax
   b. 1921 recession
   c. 100-year flood
   d. 130-30 fund

20. A _____ refers to property being sold by a taxing authority or the court to recover delinquent taxes.

When property taxes are not paid, title gets transferred to the state. The owner will then have a period of time to redeem the property by paying the overdue taxes, including penalties and costs.

   a. Tax competition
   b. Tax wedge
   c. Taxation as theft
   d. Tax Sale

21. To tax is to impose a financial charge or other levy upon a taxpayer by a state or the functional equivalent of a state.

   _____ are also imposed by many subnational entities. _____ consist of direct tax or indirect tax, and may be paid in money or as its labour equivalent (often but not always unpaid.)

   a. Taxes
   b. 1921 recession
   c. 100-year flood
   d. 130-30 fund

22. In microeconomic theory, an _____ is a graph showing different bundles of goods, each measured as to quantity, between which a consumer is indifferent. That is, at each point on the curve, the consumer has no preference for one bundle over another. In other words, they are all equally preferred.
   a. Indifference map
   b. Engel curve
   c. Expenditure minimization problem
   d. Indifference curve

23. In economics, the _____ of a good or of a service is the utility of the specific use to which an agent would put a given increase in that good or service, or of the specific use that would be abandoned in response to a given decrease. In other words, _____ is the utility of the marginal use -- which, on the assumption of economic rationality, would be the least urgent use of the good or service, from the best feasible combination of actions in which its use is included. Under the mainstream assumptions, the _____ of a good or service is the posited quantified change in utility obtained by increasing or by decreasing use of that good or service.

Chapter 10. General Equilibrium and Economic Welfare

    a. 130-30 fund
    b. 100-year flood
    c. Marginal utility
    d. 1921 recession

24. A _____ represents the combinations of goods and services that a consumer can purchase given current prices and his income. Consumer theory uses the concepts of a _____ and a preference map to analyze consumer choices. Both concepts have a ready graphical representation in the two-good case.
    a. Quality bias
    b. Revealed preference
    c. Joint demand
    d. Budget constraint

25. In economics, _____ is a measure of the relative satisfaction from consumption of various goods and services. Given this measure, one may speak meaningfully of increasing or decreasing _____, and thereby explain economic behavior in terms of attempts to increase one's _____. For illustrative purposes, changes in _____ are sometimes expressed in units called utils.
    a. Ordinal utility
    b. Utility function
    c. Expected utility hypothesis
    d. Utility

26. Given some endowment in an Edgeworth box, the _____ is the individually rational subset of the Pareto set. In other words, it is the set of Pareto efficient allocations in an economy. Also, any Walrasian equilibrium lies in the _____ of the Pareto set.
    a. Missing market
    b. Social welfare function
    c. Hidden Welfare State
    d. Contract curve

27. _____ is a common market structure where many competing producers sell products that are differentiated from one another (ie. the products are substitutes, but are not exactly alike.) Many markets are monopolistically competitive, common examples include the markets for restaurants, cereal, clothing, shoes and service industries in large cities.
    a. Monopolistic competition
    b. Financial crisis
    c. Perfect competition
    d. Mathematical economics

28. _____ are costs incurred on the purchase of land, buildings, construction and equipment to be used in the production of goods or the rendering of services. In other words, the total cost needed to bring a project to a commercially operable status. However, _____ are not limited to the initial construction of a factory or other business.
    a. Total revenue
    b. Whitemail
    c. Blanket order
    d. Capital costs

29. In economics, _____ refers to the ability of a person or a country to produce a particular good at a lower marginal cost and opportunity cost than another person or country. It is the ability to produce a product most efficiently given all the other products that could be produced. It can be contrasted with absolute advantage which refers to the ability of a person or a country to produce a particular good at a lower absolute cost than another.
    a. Triffin dilemma
    b. Gravity model of trade
    c. Comparative advantage
    d. Hot money

30. The slope of the production-possibility frontier (PPF) at any given point is called the _____. It describes numerically the rate at which one good can be transformed into the other. It is also called the (marginal) 'opportunity cost' of a commodity, that is, it is the opportunity cost of X in terms of Y at the margin.

a. Piece work
b. Productivity
c. Fordism
d. Marginal rate of transformation

31. In economics, the _____ is the rate at which a consumer is ready to give up one good in exchange for another good while maintaining the same level of satisfaction.

Under the standard assumption of neoclassical economics that goods and services are continuously divisible, the marginal rates of substitution will be the same regardless of the direction of exchange, and will correspond to the slope of an indifference curve (more precisely, to the slope multiplied by -1) passing through the consumption bundle in question, at that point: mathematically, it is the implicit derivative. MRS of Y for X is the amount of Y for which a consumer is willing to exchange for X locally.

a. Supply and demand
b. Quality bias
c. Demand vacuum
d. Marginal rate of substitution

32. _____ in economics and business is the result of an exchange and from that trade we assign a numerical monetary value to a good, service or asset. If Alice trades Bob 4 apples for an orange, the _____ of an orange is 4 apples. Inversely, the _____ of an apple is 1/4 oranges.

a. Premium pricing
b. Price war
c. Price book
d. Price

33. _____ is a common concept in economics, and gives rise to derived concepts such as consumer debt. Generally _____ is defined by opposition to production. But the precise definition can vary because different schools of economists define production quite differently.

a. Consumption
b. Foreclosure data providers
c. Federal Reserve Bank Notes
d. Cash or share options

34. An _____ is a tax levied on the financial income of people, corporations, or other legal entities. Various _____ systems exist, with varying degrees of tax incidence. Income taxation can be progressive, proportional, or regressive.

a. AD-IA Model
b. ACCRA Cost of Living Index
c. Income tax
d. ACEA agreement

35. In economics, a common-pool resource, alternatively termed a _____ resource, is a particular type of good consisting of a natural or human-made resource system, the size or characteristics of which makes it costly, but not impossible, to exclude potential beneficiaries from obtaining benefits from its use. Unlike pure public goods, common pool resources face problems of congestion or overuse, because they are subtractable. A common-pool resource typically consists of a core resource, which defines the stock variable, while providing a limited quantity of extractable fringe units, which defines the flow variable.

a. Common-pool resource
b. Price-cap regulation
c. Government monopoly
d. Common property

36. _____ is a comparison of the wealth of various members or groups in a society. It differs from the distribution of income in a manner analogous to the difference between position and speed.

Chapter 10. General Equilibrium and Economic Welfare

Wealth is a person's net worth, expressed as:

wealth = assets - liabilities

The word 'wealth' is often confused with 'income'.

a. 100-year flood
c. 130-30 fund
b. Distribution of wealth
d. Wealth condensation

37. In social choice theory, Arrow's _____ demonstrates that no voting system can convert the ranked preferences of individuals into a community-wide ranking while also meeting a certain set of reasonable criteria with three or more discrete options to choose from. These criteria are called unrestricted domain, non-imposition, non-dictatorship, Pareto efficiency, and independence of irrelevant alternatives. The theorem is often cited in discussions of election theory as it is further interpreted by the Gibbard-Satterthwaite theorem.
a. ACEA agreement
c. AD-IA Model
b. Impossibility Theorem
d. ACCRA Cost of Living Index

38. A _____ provision refers to any program which seeks to provide a minimum level of income, service or other support for many marginalized groups such as the poor, elderly, and disabled people. _____ programs are undertaken by governments as well as non-governmental organizations (NGOs.) _____ payments and services are typically provided at the expense of taxpayers generally, funded by benefactors, or by compulsory enrollment of the poor themselves.
a. Social welfare
c. 100-year flood
b. 1921 recession
d. 130-30 fund

39. In economics, a _____ is a real-valued function that ranks conceivable social states (alternative complete descriptions of the society) from lowest to highest. Inputs of the function include any variables considered to affect welfare of the society (Sen, 1970, p. 33.)
a. Frisch elasticity of labor supply
c. Social welfare function
b. Gini coefficient
d. Contract curve

40. _____ is a type of trade policy that allows traders to act and transact without interference from government. Thus, the policy permits trading partners mutual gains from trade, with goods and services produced according to the theory of comparative advantage.

Under a _____ policy, prices are a reflection of true supply and demand, and are the sole determinant of resource allocation.

a. 130-30 fund
c. 100-year flood
b. 1921 recession
d. Free Trade

41. The _____ is a trilateral trade bloc in North America created by the governments of the United States, Canada, and Mexico. The agreement creating the trade bloc came into force on January 1, 1994. It superseded the Canada-United States Free Trade Agreement between the U.S. and Canada.

a. Demand-side technologies
b. Federal Reserve Bank Notes
c. Case-Shiller Home Price Indices
d. North American Free Trade Agreement

42. The _____ is an important selective, mainly private, international organization designed by its founders to supervise and liberalize international trade. The organization officially commenced on 1 January 1995, under the Marrakesh Agreement, succeeding the 1947 General Agreement on Tariffs and Trade (GATT.)

The _____ deals with regulation of trade between participating countries; it provides a framework for negotiating and formalising trade agreements, and a dispute resolution process aimed at enforcing participants' adherence to _____ agreements which are signed by representatives of member governments and ratified by their parliaments.

a. 2009 G-20 London summit protests
b. Backus-Kehoe-Kydland consumption correlation puzzle
c. Bio-energy village
d. World Trade Organization

43. In economics, an _____ is any good (e.g. a commodity) or service brought into one country from another country in a legitimate fashion, typically for use in trade.It is a good that is brought in from another country for sale. _____ goods or services are provided to domestic consumers by foreign producers. An _____ in the receiving country is an export to the sending country.

a. Import
b. Economic integration
c. Incoterms
d. Import quota

44. _____ is subcontracting a process, such as product design or manufacturing, to a third-party company. The decision to outsource is often made in the interest of lowering cost or making better use of time and energy costs, redirecting or conserving energy directed at the competencies of a particular business, or to make more efficient use of land, labor, capital, (information) technology and resources. _____ became part of the business lexicon during the 1980s.

a. Averch-Johnson effect
b. Additional Funds Needed
c. Outsourcing
d. Electronic business

45. The Court of Justice of the European Communities, usually called the _____, is the highest court in the European Union in matters of European Community law. It has the ultimate say on matters of EU law in order to ensure its equal application across all EU member states.

The court was established in 1952 and is -- unlike most other Union institutions -- based in Luxembourg.

a. ACEA agreement
b. ACCRA Cost of Living Index
c. European Court of Justice
d. European Union

46. The _____ is an economic and political union of 27 member states, located primarily in Europe. It was established by the Treaty of Maastricht on 1 November 1993, upon the foundations of the pre-existing European Economic Community. With a population of almost 500 million, the _____ generates an estimated 30% share (US$18.4 trillion in 2008) of the nominal gross world product.

a. ACCRA Cost of Living Index
b. ACEA agreement
c. European Court of Justice
d. European Union

47. _____ is a program of the United States Department of Labor that provides a variety of reemployment services and benefits to workers who have lost their jobs or suffered a reduction of hours and wages as a result of increased imports or shifts in production outside the United States. The _____ program aims to help program participants obtain new jobs, ensuring they retain employment and earn wages comparable to their prior employment.

_____ was established as part of the Trade Expansion Act in 1962, during the Presidency of John F. Kennedy.

a. Delancey Street Foundation
b. New Economic Policy
c. Financial Crimes Enforcement Network
d. Trade Adjustment Assistance

Chapter 11. Monopoly

1. Economics:

    • _____, the desire to own something and the ability to pay for it
    • _____ curve, a graphic representation of a _____ schedule
    • _____ deposit, the money in checking accounts
    • _____ pull theory, the theory that inflation occurs when _____ for goods and services exceeds existing supplies
    • _____ schedule, a table that lists the quantity of a good a person will buy it each different price
    • _____ side economics, the school of economics at believes government spending and tax cuts open economy by raising _____

    a. McKesson ' Robbins scandal   b. Demand
    c. Variability   d. Production

2. In economics, the _____ can be defined as the graph depicting the relationship between the price of a certain commodity, and the amount of it that consumers are willing and able to purchase at that given price. It is a graphic representation of a demand schedule. The _____ for all consumers together follows from the _____ of every individual consumer: the individual demands at each price are added together.
    a. Cost curve   b. Wage curve
    c. Kuznets curve   d. Demand curve

3. An _____ is a tax levied on the financial income of people, corporations, or other legal entities. Various _____ systems exist, with varying degrees of tax incidence. Income taxation can be progressive, proportional, or regressive.
    a. ACCRA Cost of Living Index   b. AD-IA Model
    c. ACEA agreement   d. Income tax

4. In economics, _____ is the ability of a firm to alter the market price of a good or service. A firm with _____ can raise prices without losing all customers to competitors.

    When a firm has _____ it faces a downward-sloping demand curve.

    a. Revenue-cap regulation   b. Market power
    c. Price makers   d. Pacman conjecture

5. In economics, a _____ exists when a specific individual or enterprise has sufficient control over a particular product or service to determine significantly the terms on which other individuals shall have access to it. Monopolies are thus characterized by a lack of economic competition for the good or service that they provide and a lack of viable substitute goods. The verb 'monopolize' refers to the process by which a firm gains persistently greater market share than what is expected under perfect competition.
    a. Monopoly   b. 1921 recession
    c. 100-year flood   d. 130-30 fund

6. In economics, a firm is said to reap _____s when a lack of viable market competition allows it to set its prices above the equilibrium price for a good or service without losing profits to competitors. _____ is a type of economic profit, that is, it is a profit greater than the normal profit that is typical in a perfectly competitive industry. The resulting price is known as the monopoly price.

a. Monopoly profit
c. First-price sealed-bid auction
b. Cleanup clause
d. Borrowing base

7. In economics, _____ is the process by which a firm determines the price and output level that returns the greatest profit. There are several approaches to this problem. The total revenue--total cost method relies on the fact that profit equals revenue minus cost, and the marginal revenue--marginal cost method is based on the fact that total profit in a perfectly competitive market reaches its maximum point where marginal revenue equals marginal cost.
   a. 100-year flood
   c. Profit maximization
   b. Profit margin
   d. Normal profit

8. A _____ is a consumption tax charged at the point of purchase for certain goods and services. The tax is usually set as a percentage by the government charging the tax. There is usually a list of exemptions.
   a. 1921 recession
   c. 130-30 fund
   b. Sales tax
   d. 100-year flood

9. To _____ is to impose a financial charge or other levy upon a taxpayer by a state or the functional equivalent of a state.

   _____es are also imposed by many subnational entities. _____es consist of direct _____ or indirect _____, and may be paid in money or as its labour equivalent (often but not always unpaid.)

   a. 1921 recession
   c. 100-year flood
   b. 130-30 fund
   d. Tax

10. To tax is to impose a financial charge or other levy upon a taxpayer by a state or the functional equivalent of a state.

    _____ are also imposed by many subnational entities. _____ consist of direct tax or indirect tax, and may be paid in money or as its labour equivalent (often but not always unpaid.)

    a. Taxes
    c. 100-year flood
    b. 1921 recession
    d. 130-30 fund

11. In economics, a common-pool resource, alternatively termed a _____ resource, is a particular type of good consisting of a natural or human-made resource system, the size or characteristics of which makes it costly, but not impossible, to exclude potential beneficiaries from obtaining benefits from its use. Unlike pure public goods, common pool resources face problems of congestion or overuse, because they are subtractable. A common-pool resource typically consists of a core resource, which defines the stock variable, while providing a limited quantity of extractable fringe units, which defines the flow variable.
    a. Common property
    c. Price-cap regulation
    b. Government monopoly
    d. Common-pool resource

12. In microeconomics, _____ is quite simply the conversion of inputs into outputs. It is an economic process that uses resources to create a good or service that is suitable for exchange. This can include manufacturing, storing, shipping, and packaging.

Chapter 11. Monopoly

    a. Solved
    c. MET

    b. Red Guards
    d. Production

13. In microeconomics, _____ is the extra revenue that an additional unit of product will bring. It is the additional income from selling one more unit of a good; sometimes equal to price. It can also be described as the change in total revenue/change in number of units sold.

    a. Reservation price
    c. Long term

    b. Market demand schedule
    d. Marginal revenue

14. _____ in economics and business is the result of an exchange and from that trade we assign a numerical monetary value to a good, service or asset. If Alice trades Bob 4 apples for an orange, the _____ of an orange is 4 apples. Inversely, the _____ of an apple is 1/4 oranges.

    a. Premium pricing
    c. Price war

    b. Price book
    d. Price

15. _____ exists when sales of identical goods or services are transacted at different prices from the same provider. In a theoretical market with perfect information, no transaction costs or prohibition on secondary exchange (or re-selling) to prevent arbitrage, _____ can only be a feature of monopoly and oligopoly markets, where market power can be exercised. Otherwise, the moment the seller tries to sell the same good at different prices, the buyer at the lower price can arbitrage by selling to the consumer buying at the higher price but with a tiny discount.

    a. Lerner Index
    c. Transfer pricing

    b. Loss leader
    d. Price discrimination

16. _____ is defined as the measure of responsiveness in the quantity demanded for a commodity as a result of change in price of the same commodity. It is a measure of how consumers react to a change in price. In other words, it is percentage change in quantity demanded as per the percentage change in price of the same commodity.

    a. 100-year flood
    c. 1921 recession

    b. 130-30 fund
    d. Price elasticity of demand

17. A _____ is a situation that involves losing one quality or aspect of something in return for gaining another quality or aspect. It implies a decision to be made with full comprehension of both the upside and downside of a particular choice.

In economics the term is expressed as opportunity cost, referring the most preferred alternative given up.

    a. Trade-off
    c. Nonmarket

    b. Friedman-Savage utility function
    d. Whitemail

18. In finance, a _____ is a debt security, in which the authorized issuer owes the holders a debt and, depending on the terms of the _____, is obliged to pay interest (the coupon) and/or to repay the principal at a later date, termed maturity. A _____ is a formal contract to repay borrowed money with interest at fixed intervals.

Thus a _____ is like a loan: the issuer is the borrower (debtor), the holder is the lender (creditor), and the coupon is the interest.

Chapter 11. Monopoly

a. Zero-coupon
b. Callable
c. Prize Bond
d. Bond

19. In economics, _____ is the ratio of the percent change in one variable to the percent change in another variable. It is a tool for measuring the responsiveness of a function to changes in parameters in a relative way. Commonly analyzed are _____ of substitution, price and wealth.
   a. Elasticity of demand
   b. Elasticity
   c. ACEA agreement
   d. ACCRA Cost of Living Index

20. Price _____ is defined as the measure of responsiveness in the quantity demanded for a commodity as a result of change in price of the same commodity. It is a measure of how consumers react to a change in price. In other words, it is percentage change in quantity demanded by the percentage change in price of the same commodity.
   a. Elasticity of demand
   b. Elasticity
   c. ACCRA Cost of Living Index
   d. ACEA agreement

21. _____ is one of the four Ps of the marketing mix. The other three aspects are product, promotion, and place. It is also a key variable in microeconomic price allocation theory.
   a. Guaranteed Maximum Price
   b. Point of total assumption
   c. Premium pricing
   d. Pricing

22. In microeconomics, _____ is the term used to refer to total when marginal cost is subtracted from marginal revenue. Under the marginal approach to profit maximization, to maximize profits, a firm should continue to produce a good until _____ is zero. Profit Maximization - The Marginal Approach.
   a. Corporate synergy
   b. Marginal profit
   c. Holding period return
   d. Lehman scale

23. A _____ is a counterfeit agreement among industries. It is an informal organization of producers that agree to coordinate prices and production. _____s usually occur in an oligopolistic industry, where there is a small number of sellers and usually involve homogeneous products.
   a. 100-year flood
   b. Shill
   c. Shanzhai
   d. Cartel

24. _____ is the transition of a national economy from monopoly control by groups of large businesses to a free market economy. This change rarely arises naturally, and is generally the result of regulation by a governing body.

A modern example of _____ is the economic restructuring of Germany after the fall of the Third Reich in 1945.

   a. Complementary monopoly
   b. Decartelization
   c. Monopolization
   d. Market power

25. _____s is the social science that studies the production, distribution, and consumption of goods and services. The term _____s comes from the Ancient Greek oá¼°κονομῖα from oá¼¶κος (oikos, 'house') + νÏŒμος (nomos, 'custom' or 'law'), hence 'rules of the house(hold)'. Current _____ models developed out of the broader field of political economy in the late 19th century, owing to a desire to use an empirical approach more akin to the physical sciences.

a. Inflation
b. Opportunity cost
c. Energy economics
d. Economic

26. The _____ describes a firm's market power. It is defined by:

$$L = \frac{P - MC}{P}$$

where P is the market price set by the firm and MC is the firm's marginal cost. The index ranges from a high of 1 to a low of 0, with higher numbers implying greater market power.

a. Break even analysis
b. Lerner Index
c. Two-part tariff
d. Discounts and allowances

27. In economics and finance, _____ is the change in total cost that arises when the quantity produced changes by one unit. It is the cost of producing one more unit of a good. Mathematically, the _____ function is expressed as the first derivative of the total cost (TC) function with respect to quantity (Q.)

a. Quality costs
b. Khozraschyot
c. Variable cost
d. Marginal cost

28. In economics, a _____ is a graph of the costs of production as a function of total quantity produced. In a free market economy, productively efficient firms use these curves to find the optimal point of production, where they make the most profits. There are a few different types of _____ s, each relevant to a different area of economics.

a. Cost curve
b. Phillips curve
c. Demand curve
d. Kuznets curve

29. In economics, _____ is equal to total cost divided by the number of goods produced (the output quantity, Q.) It is also equal to the sum of average variable costs (total variable costs divided by Q) plus average fixed costs (total fixed costs divided by Q.) _____ s may be dependent on the time period considered (increasing production may be expensive or impossible in the short term, for example.)

a. Average variable cost
b. Average fixed cost
c. Explicit cost
d. Average cost

30. The _____ consists of a number of economic theories which describe the nature of the firm, company including its existence, its behaviour, and its relationship with the market.

In simplified terms, the _____ aims to answer these questions:

1. Existence - why do firms emerge, why are not all transactions in the economy mediated over the market?
2. Boundaries - why the boundary between firms and the market is located exactly there? Which transactions are performed internally and which are negotiated on the market?
3. Organization - why are firms structured in such specific way? What is the interplay of formal and informal relationships?

Chapter 11. Monopoly

Despite looking simple, these questions are not answered by the established economic theory, which usually views firms as given, and treats them as black boxes without any internal structure.

The First World War period saw a change of emphasis in economic theory away from industry-level analysis which mainly included analysing markets to analysis at the level of the firm, as it became increasingly clear that perfect competition was no longer an adequate model of how firms behaved. Economic theory till then had focussed on trying to understand markets alone and there had been little study on understanding why firms or organisations exist.

   a. Policy Ineffectiveness Proposition
   b. Technology gap
   c. Khazzoom-Brookes postulate
   d. Theory of the firm

31. In economics, a _____ is a loss of economic efficiency that can occur when equilibrium for a good or service is not Pareto optimal. In other words, either people who would have more marginal benefit than marginal cost are not buying the good or service, or people who would have more marginal cost than marginal benefit are buying the product.

Causes of _____ can include monopoly pricing, externalities, taxes or subsidies, and binding price ceilings or floors.

   a. Distributive efficiency
   b. Leapfrogging
   c. Contract curve
   d. Deadweight loss

32. An _____ is a tax based on the value of real estate or personal property. It is more common than the opposite, a specific duty, or a tax based on the quantity of an item regardless of price.

An _____ is typically imposed at the time of a transaction), but it may be imposed on an annual basis (real or personal property tax) or in connection with another significant event (inheritance tax, surrendering citizenship, or tariffs.)

   a. Optimal tax
   b. Indirect tax
   c. User charge
   d. Ad valorem tax

33. A _____ is a duty imposed on goods when they are moved across a political boundary. They are usually associated with protectionism, the economic policy of restraining trade between nations. For political reasons, _____s are usually imposed on imported goods, although they may also be imposed on exported goods.
   a. 130-30 fund
   b. 1921 recession
   c. 100-year flood
   d. Tariff

34. _____ was the American founder of the Ford Motor Company and father of modern assembly lines used in mass production. His introduction of the Model T automobile revolutionized transportation and American industry. He was a prolific inventor and was awarded 161 U.S. patents.
   a. Henry Ford
   b. Werner Sombart
   c. George Cabot Lodge II
   d. Maximilian Carl Emil Weber

35. _____ are conceptually similar to economies of scale. Whereas economies of scale primarily refer to efficiencies associated with supply-side changes, such as increasing or decreasing the scale of production, of a single product type, _____ refer to efficiencies primarily associated with demand-side changes, such as increasing or decreasing the scope of marketing and distribution, of different types of products. _____ are one of the main reasons for such marketing strategies as product bundling, product lining, and family branding.

   a. Economies of scope
   b. Isoquant
   c. Economic production quantity
   d. Economies of scale

36. _____, in microeconomics, are the cost advantages that a business obtains due to expansion. They are factors that cause a producere;s average cost per unit to fall as scale is increased. _____ is a long run concept and refers to reductions in unit cost as the size of a facility, or scale, increases.

   a. Economic production quantity
   b. Isoquant
   c. Economies of scale
   d. Underinvestment employment relationship

37. A public utility (usually just utility) is an organization that maintains the infrastructure for a public service (often also providing a service using that infrastructure.) _____ are subject to forms of public control and regulation ranging from local community-based groups to state-wide government monopolies. Common arguments in favor of regulation include the desire to control market power, facilitate competition, promote investment or system expansion, or stabilize markets.

   a. 1921 recession
   b. 100-year flood
   c. 130-30 fund
   d. Public utilities

38. In economics and sociology, an _____ is any factor (financial or non-financial) that enables or motivates a particular course of action, or counts as a reason for preferring one choice to the alternatives. It is an expectation that encourages people to behave in a certain way. Since human beings are purposeful creatures, the study of _____ structures is central to the study of all economic activity (both in terms of individual decision-making and in terms of co-operation and competition within a larger institutional structure.)

   a. Isocost
   b. Epstein-Zin preferences
   c. Economic reform
   d. Incentive

39. A _____ is a set of exclusive rights granted by a state to an inventor or his assignee for a limited period of time in exchange for a disclosure of an invention.

The procedure for granting _____s, the requirements placed on the _____ee and the extent of the exclusive rights vary widely between countries according to national laws and international agreements. Typically, however, a _____ application must include one or more claims defining the invention which must be new, inventive, and useful or industrially applicable.

   a. Bank regulation
   b. Bona fide occupational qualification
   c. Long service leave
   d. Patent

40. _____ are legal property rights over creations of the mind, both artistic and commercial, and the corresponding fields of law. Under _____ law, owners are granted certain exclusive rights to a variety of intangible assets, such as musical, literary, and artistic works; ideas, discoveries and inventions; and words, phrases, symbols, and designs. Common types of _____ include copyrights, trademarks, patents, industrial design rights and trade secrets.

Chapter 11. Monopoly

a. Intellectual property
b. Expedited Funds Availability Act
c. Ease of Doing Business Index
d. Independent contractor

41. A _____ is the exclusive authority to determine how a resource is used, whether that resource is owned by government or by individuals. All economic goods have a _____s attribute. This attribute has three broad components

1. The right to use the good
2. The right to earn income from the good
3. The right to transfer the good to others

The concept of _____s as used by economists and legal scholars are related but distinct. The distinction is largely seen in the economists' focus on the ability of an individual or collective to control the use of the good.

a. High-reeve
b. Holder in due course
c. Post-sale restraint
d. Property right

42. A _____ is a government imposed limit on how high a price can be charged on a product. For a _____ to be effective, it must differ from the free market price. In the graph at right, the supply and demand curves intersect to determine the free-market quantity and price.

a. Product sabotage
b. Pricing
c. Price ceiling
d. Fire sale

43. The _____ is an important selective, mainly private, international organization designed by its founders to supervise and liberalize international trade. The organization officially commenced on 1 January 1995, under the Marrakesh Agreement, succeeding the 1947 General Agreement on Tariffs and Trade (GATT.)

The _____ deals with regulation of trade between participating countries; it provides a framework for negotiating and formalising trade agreements, and a dispute resolution process aimed at enforcing participants' adherence to _____ agreements which are signed by representatives of member governments and ratified by their parliaments.

a. 2009 G-20 London summit protests
b. World Trade Organization
c. Backus-Kehoe-Kydland consumption correlation puzzle
d. Bio-energy village

44. _____ and behavioral finance are closely related fields that have evolved to be a separate branch of economic and financial analysis which applies scientific research on human and social, cognitive and emotional factors to better understand economic decisions by consumers, borrowers, investors, and how they affect market prices, returns and the allocation of resources.

The field is primarily concerned with the bounds of rationality (selfishness, self-control) of economic agents. Behavioral models typically integrate insights from psychology with neo-classical economic theory.

a. Neoclassical economics
b. Georgism
c. Behavioral economics
d. Mainstream economics

Chapter 11. Monopoly

45. In economics, an _____ is any good or commodity, transported from one country to another country in a legitimate fashion, typically for use in trade. _____ goods or services are provided to foreign consumers by domestic producers. _____ is an important part of international trade.
   a. Export
   b. AD-IA Model
   c. ACCRA Cost of Living Index
   d. ACEA agreement

46. _____ is the observation that people often do and believe things because many other people do and believe the same things. The effect is often pejoratively called herding instinct, particularly when applied to adolescents. People tend to follow the crowd without examining the merits of a particular thing.
   a. Hyperbolic discounting
   b. Bandwagon effect
   c. Halo effect
   d. Sunk costs

Chapter 12. Pricing

1. Economics:

   - _____, the desire to own something and the ability to pay for it
   - _____ curve, a graphic representation of a _____ schedule
   - _____ deposit, the money in checking accounts
   - _____ pull theory, the theory that inflation occurs when _____ for goods and services exceeds existing supplies
   - _____ schedule, a table that lists the quantity of a good a person will buy it each different price
   - _____ side economics, the school of economics at believes government spending and tax cuts open economy by raising _____

   a. McKesson ' Robbins scandal   b. Demand
   c. Production   d. Variability

2. In economics, the _____ can be defined as the graph depicting the relationship between the price of a certain commodity, and the amount of it that consumers are willing and able to purchase at that given price. It is a graphic representation of a demand schedule. The _____ for all consumers together follows from the _____ of every individual consumer: the individual demands at each price are added together.

   a. Kuznets curve   b. Wage curve
   c. Demand curve   d. Cost curve

3. _____ in economics and business is the result of an exchange and from that trade we assign a numerical monetary value to a good, service or asset. If Alice trades Bob 4 apples for an orange, the _____ of an orange is 4 apples. Inversely, the _____ of an apple is 1/4 oranges.

   a. Price war   b. Price
   c. Premium pricing   d. Price book

4. _____ exists when sales of identical goods or services are transacted at different prices from the same provider. In a theoretical market with perfect information, no transaction costs or prohibition on secondary exchange (or re-selling) to prevent arbitrage, _____ can only be a feature of monopoly and oligopoly markets, where market power can be exercised. Otherwise, the moment the seller tries to sell the same good at different prices, the buyer at the lower price can arbitrage by selling to the consumer buying at the higher price but with a tiny discount.

   a. Lerner Index   b. Price discrimination
   c. Transfer pricing   d. Loss leader

5. To _____ is to impose a financial charge or other levy upon a taxpayer by a state or the functional equivalent of a state.

   _____es are also imposed by many subnational entities. _____es consist of direct _____ or indirect _____, and may be paid in money or as its labour equivalent (often but not always unpaid.)

   a. 1921 recession   b. 100-year flood
   c. Tax   d. 130-30 fund

6. To tax is to impose a financial charge or other levy upon a taxpayer by a state or the functional equivalent of a state.

_____ are also imposed by many subnational entities. _____ consist of direct tax or indirect tax, and may be paid in money or as its labour equivalent (often but not always unpaid.)

    a. 100-year flood
    b. Taxes
    c. 1921 recession
    d. 130-30 fund

7. A _____ is a price discrimination technique in which the price of a product or service is composed of two parts - a lump-sum fee as well as a per-unit charge. In general, price discrimination techniques only occur in partially or fully monopolistic markets. It is designed to enable the firm to capture more consumer surplus than it otherwise would in a non-discriminating pricing environment.
    a. Big ticket item
    b. Penetration pricing
    c. Price floor
    d. Two-part tariff

8. _____ is one of the four Ps of the marketing mix. The other three aspects are product, promotion, and place. It is also a key variable in microeconomic price allocation theory.
    a. Pricing
    b. Point of total assumption
    c. Guaranteed Maximum Price
    d. Premium pricing

9. A _____ is a duty imposed on goods when they are moved across a political boundary. They are usually associated with protectionism, the economic policy of restraining trade between nations. For political reasons, _____s are usually imposed on imported goods, although they may also be imposed on exported goods.
    a. 130-30 fund
    b. 1921 recession
    c. 100-year flood
    d. Tariff

10. _____ is a broad label that refers to any individuals or households that use goods and services generated within the economy. The concept of a _____ is used in different contexts, so that the usage and significance of the term may vary.

Typically when business people and economists talk of _____s they are talking about person as _____, an aggregated commodity item with little individuality other than that expressed in the buy/not-buy decision.

    a. 130-30 fund
    b. Consumer
    c. 1921 recession
    d. 100-year flood

11. The term surplus is used in economics for several related quantities. The _____ is the amount that consumers benefit by being able to purchase a product for a price that is less than they would be willing to pay. The producer surplus is the amount that producers benefit by selling at a market price mechanism that is higher than they would be willing to sell for.
    a. Necessity good
    b. Consumer surplus
    c. Microeconomic reform
    d. Marginal rate of technical substitution

12. The _____ describes a firm's market power. It is defined by:

$$L = \frac{P - MC}{P}$$

where P is the market price set by the firm and MC is the firm's marginal cost. The index ranges from a high of 1 to a low of 0, with higher numbers implying greater market power.

    a. Lerner Index
    c. Discounts and allowances
    b. Break even analysis
    d. Two-part tariff

13. In microeconomics, _____ is the extra revenue that an additional unit of product will bring. It is the additional income from selling one more unit of a good; sometimes equal to price. It can also be described as the change in total revenue/change in number of units sold.

    a. Market demand schedule
    c. Reservation price
    b. Marginal revenue
    d. Long term

14. In economics, a _____ is a loss of economic efficiency that can occur when equilibrium for a good or service is not Pareto optimal. In other words, either people who would have more marginal benefit than marginal cost are not buying the good or service, or people who would have more marginal cost than marginal benefit are buying the product.

Causes of _____ can include monopoly pricing, externalities, taxes or subsidies, and binding price ceilings or floors.

    a. Leapfrogging
    c. Contract curve
    b. Deadweight loss
    d. Distributive efficiency

15. _____ or economic opportunity loss is the value of the next best alternative foregone as the result of making a decision. _____ analysis is an important part of a company's decision-making processes but is not treated as an actual cost in any financial statement. The next best thing that a person can engage in is referred to as the _____ of doing the best thing and ignoring the next best thing to be done.

    a. Opportunity cost
    c. Industrial organization
    b. Economic
    d. Economic ideology

16. In economics and related disciplines, a _____ is a cost incurred in making an economic exchange. For example, most people, when buying or selling a stock, must pay a commission to their broker; that commission is a _____ of doing the stock deal. Or consider buying a banana from a store; to purchase the banana, your costs will be not only the price of the banana itself, but also the energy and effort it requires to find out which of the various banana products you prefer, where to get them and at what price, the cost of traveling from your house to the store and back, the time waiting in line, and the effort of the paying itself; the costs above and beyond the cost of the banana are the _____s.

    a. Cost of poor quality
    c. Sliding scale fees
    b. Cost allocation
    d. Transaction cost

17. A trade union or _____ is an organization of workers who have banded together to achieve common goals in key areas and working conditions. The trade union, through its leadership, bargains with the employer on behalf of union members (rank and file members) and negotiates labor contracts (Collective bargaining) with employers. This may include the negotiation of wages, work rules, complaint procedures, rules governing hiring, firing and promotion of workers, benefits, workplace safety and policies.

a. Demand-side technologies
b. Basis of futures
c. Labor union
d. Business valuation standards

18. A _____ or labor union is an organization of workers who have banded together to achieve common goals in key areas and working conditions. The _____, through its leadership, bargains with the employer on behalf of union members (rank and file members) and negotiates labor contracts (Collective bargaining) with employers. This may include the negotiation of wages, work rules, complaint procedures, rules governing hiring, firing and promotion of workers, benefits, workplace safety and policies.
    a. Consumer goods
    b. Case-Shiller Home Price Indices
    c. Trade union
    d. Guaranteed investment contracts

19. A public utility (usually just utility) is an organization that maintains the infrastructure for a public service (often also providing a service using that infrastructure.) _____ are subject to forms of public control and regulation ranging from local community-based groups to state-wide government monopolies. Common arguments in favor of regulation include the desire to control market power, facilitate competition, promote investment or system expansion, or stabilize markets.
    a. Public utilities
    b. 1921 recession
    c. 130-30 fund
    d. 100-year flood

20. A _____ is a place of residence or refuge and comfort. It is usually a place in which an individual or a family can rest and be able to store personal property. Most modern-day households contain sanitary facilities and a means of preparing food.
    a. 130-30 fund
    b. 1921 recession
    c. Home
    d. 100-year flood

21. In economics, _____ is equal to total cost divided by the number of goods produced (the output quantity, Q.) It is also equal to the sum of average variable costs (total variable costs divided by Q) plus average fixed costs (total fixed costs divided by Q.) _____s may be dependent on the time period considered (increasing production may be expensive or impossible in the short term, for example.)
    a. Explicit cost
    b. Average variable cost
    c. Average cost
    d. Average fixed cost

22. In economics, a _____ is a graph of the costs of production as a function of total quantity produced. In a free market economy, productively efficient firms use these curves to find the optimal point of production, where they make the most profits. There are a few different types of _____s, each relevant to a different area of economics.
    a. Kuznets curve
    b. Phillips curve
    c. Demand curve
    d. Cost curve

23. _____ refers to a business or organization attempting to acquire goods or services to accomplish the goals of the enterprise. Though there are several organizations that attempt to set standards in the _____ process, processes can vary greatly between organizations. Typically the word '_____' is not used interchangeably with the word 'procurement', since procurement typically includes Expediting, Supplier Quality, and Traffic and Logistics (T'L) in addition to _____.
    a. Purchasing
    b. 130-30 fund
    c. 100-year flood
    d. Free port

Chapter 12. Pricing

24. _____ is an economic model used to describe an industry structure in which companies compete on the amount of output they will produce, which they decide on independently of each other and at the same time. It is named after Antoine Augustin Cournot (1801-1877) after he observed competition in a spring water duopoly. It has the following features:

- There is more than one firm and all firms produce a homogeneous product, i.e. there is no product differentiation;
- Firms do not cooperate, i.e. there is no collusion;
- Firms have market power, i.e. each firm's output decision affects the good's price;
- The number of firms is fixed;
- Firms compete in quantities, and choose quantities simultaneously;
- The firms are economically rational and act strategically, usually seeking to maximize profit given their competitors' decisions.

An essential assumption of this model is that each firm aims to maximize profits, based on the expectation that its own output decision will not have an effect on the decisions of its rivals. Price is a commonly known decreasing function of total output.

 a. Cournot competition
 c. 1921 recession
 b. 100-year flood
 d. 130-30 fund

25. _____ is a common market structure where many competing producers sell products that are differentiated from one another (ie. the products are substitutes, but are not exactly alike.) Many markets are monopolistically competitive, common examples include the markets for restaurants, cereal, clothing, shoes and service industries in large cities.

 a. Mathematical economics
 c. Perfect competition
 b. Financial crisis
 d. Monopolistic competition

26. A _____ is a tool used in industrial business-to-business procurement. It is a type of auction in which the role of the buyer and seller are reversed, with the primary objective to drive purchase prices downward. In an ordinary auction, buyers compete to obtain a good or service.

 a. Demand-side
 c. CPFR
 b. Demand side
 d. Reverse auction

27. _____ is an offer (often competitive) of setting a price one is willing to pay for something. A price offer is called a bid. The term may be used in context of auctions, stock exchange, card games, or real estate transactions.

 a. Central limit order book
 c. Bidding
 b. Bord halfpenny
 d. Normal good

Chapter 13. Oligopoly and Monopolistic Competition

1. The _____ consists of a number of economic theories which describe the nature of the firm, company including its existence, its behaviour, and its relationship with the market.

In simplified terms, the _____ aims to answer these questions:

1. Existence - why do firms emerge, why are not all transactions in the economy mediated over the market?
2. Boundaries - why the boundary between firms and the market is located exactly there? Which transactions are performed internally and which are negotiated on the market?
3. Organization - why are firms structured in such specific way? What is the interplay of formal and informal relationships?

Despite looking simple, these questions are not answered by the established economic theory, which usually views firms as given, and treats them as black boxes without any internal structure.

The First World War period saw a change of emphasis in economic theory away from industry-level analysis which mainly included analysing markets to analysis at the level of the firm, as it became increasingly clear that perfect competition was no longer an adequate model of how firms behaved. Economic theory till then had focussed on trying to understand markets alone and there had been little study on understanding why firms or organisations exist.

a. Technology gap
b. Policy Ineffectiveness Proposition
c. Khazzoom-Brookes postulate
d. Theory of the firm

2. In economics, a _____ exists when the production or use of goods and services by the market is not efficient. That is, there exists another outcome where all involved can be made better off. _____s can be viewed as scenarios where individuals' pursuit of pure self-interest leads to results that are not efficient - that can be improved upon from the societal point-of-view.

a. Fixed exchange rate
b. General equilibrium
c. Financial economics
d. Market failure

3. _____ is a common market structure where many competing producers sell products that are differentiated from one another (ie. the products are substitutes, but are not exactly alike.) Many markets are monopolistically competitive, common examples include the markets for restaurants, cereal, clothing, shoes and service industries in large cities.

a. Mathematical economics
b. Financial crisis
c. Monopolistic competition
d. Perfect competition

4. A _____ is a counterfeit agreement among industries. It is an informal organization of producers that agree to coordinate prices and production. _____s usually occur in an oligopolistic industry, where there is a small number of sellers and usually involve homogeneous products.

a. 100-year flood
b. Shanzhai
c. Shill
d. Cartel

5. _____ is the transition of a national economy from monopoly control by groups of large businesses to a free market economy. This change rarely arises naturally, and is generally the result of regulation by a governing body.

A modern example of _____ is the economic restructuring of Germany after the fall of the Third Reich in 1945.

  a. Market power
  b. Decartelization
  c. Complementary monopoly
  d. Monopolization

6. Necessary _____s:

If x is a necessary _____ of y, then the presence of y necessarily implies the presence of x. The presence of x, however, does not imply that y will occur.

Sufficient _____s:

If x is a sufficient _____ of y, then the presence of x necessarily implies the presence of y.

  a. Cause
  b. Political philosophy
  c. Materialism
  d. Philosophy of economics

7. _____ are conceptually similar to economies of scale. Whereas economies of scale primarily refer to efficiencies associated with supply-side changes, such as increasing or decreasing the scale of production, of a single product type, _____ refer to efficiencies primarily associated with demand-side changes, such as increasing or decreasing the scope of marketing and distribution, of different types of products. _____ are one of the main reasons for such marketing strategies as product bundling, product lining, and family branding.
  a. Economic production quantity
  b. Economies of scale
  c. Isoquant
  d. Economies of scope

8. _____ is one of the four Ps of the marketing mix. The other three aspects are product, promotion, and place. It is also a key variable in microeconomic price allocation theory.
  a. Point of total assumption
  b. Guaranteed Maximum Price
  c. Premium pricing
  d. Pricing

9. Competitive market equilibrium is the traditional concept of economic equilibrium, appropriate for the analysis of commodity markets with flexible prices and many traders, and serving as the benchmark of efficiency in economic analysis. It relies crucially on the assumption of a competitive environment where each trader decides upon a quantity that is so small compared to the total quantity traded in the market that their individual transactions have no influence on the prices. Competitive markets are an ideal, a standard that other market structures are evaluated by.

A _____ consists of a vector of prices and an allocation such that given the prices, each trader by maximizing his objective function (profit, preferences) subject to his technological possibilities and resource constraints plans to trade into his part of the proposed allocation, and such that the prices make all net trades compatible with one another ('clear the market') by equating aggregate supply and demand for the commodities which are traded.

a. Product-Market Growth Matrix
b. Market system
c. Partial equilibrium
d. Competitive equilibrium

10. _____ is an economic model used to describe an industry structure in which companies compete on the amount of output they will produce, which they decide on independently of each other and at the same time. It is named after Antoine Augustin Cournot (1801-1877) after he observed competition in a spring water duopoly. It has the following features:

- There is more than one firm and all firms produce a homogeneous product, i.e. there is no product differentiation;
- Firms do not cooperate, i.e. there is no collusion;
- Firms have market power, i.e. each firm's output decision affects the good's price;
- The number of firms is fixed;
- Firms compete in quantities, and choose quantities simultaneously;
- The firms are economically rational and act strategically, usually seeking to maximize profit given their competitors' decisions.

An essential assumption of this model is that each firm aims to maximize profits, based on the expectation that its own output decision will not have an effect on the decisions of its rivals. Price is a commonly known decreasing function of total output.

a. 1921 recession
b. 100-year flood
c. Cournot competition
d. 130-30 fund

11. _____ is a branch of applied mathematics that is used in the social sciences (most notably economics), biology, engineering, political science, international relations, computer science, and philosophy. _____ attempts to mathematically capture behavior in strategic situations, in which an individual's success in making choices depends on the choices of others. While initially developed to analyze competitions in which one individual does better at another's expense (zero sum games), it has been expanded to treat a wide class of interactions, which are classified according to several criteria.
a. Game theory
b. Dollar auction
c. Proper equilibrium
d. Discriminatory price auction

12. _____ theory is a branch of theoretical economics. It seeks to explain the behavior of supply, demand and prices in a whole economy with several or many markets. It is often assumed that agents are price takers and in that setting two common notions of equilibrium exist: Walrasian (or competitive) equilibrium, and its generalization; a price equilibrium with transfers.
a. Human capital
b. Rational choice theory
c. New Keynesian economics
d. General equilibrium

13. In economics, economic equilibrium is simply a state of the world where economic forces are balanced and in the absence of external influences the (equilibrium) values of economic variables will not change. It is the point at which quantity demanded and quantity supplied are equal. _____, for example, refers to a condition where a market price is established through competition such that the amount of goods or services sought by buyers is equal to the amount of goods or services produced by sellers.
a. Marketization
b. Product-Market Growth Matrix
c. Regulated market
d. Market equilibrium

Chapter 13. Oligopoly and Monopolistic Competition

14. In economics, _____ describes the state of a market with respect to competition.

- Perfect competition, in which the market consists of a very large number of firms producing a homogeneous product.
- Monopolistic competition where there are a large number of independent firms which have a very small proportion of the market share.
- Oligopoly, in which a market is dominated by a small number of firms which own more than 40% of the market share.
- Oligopsony, a market dominated by many sellers and a few buyers.
- Monopoly, where there is only one provider of a product or service.
- Natural monopoly, a monopoly in which economies of scale cause efficiency to increase continuously with the size of the firm. A firm is a natural monopoly if it is able to serve the entire market demand at a lower cost than any combination of two or more smaller, more specialized firms.
- Monopsony, when there is only one buyer in a market.

The imperfectly competitive structure is quite identical to the realistic market conditions where some monopolistic competitors, monopolists, oligopolists, and duopolists exist and dominate the market conditions. The elements of _____ include the number and size distribution of firms, entry conditions, and the extent of differentiation.

These somewhat abstract concerns tend to determine some but not all details of a specific concrete market system where buyers and sellers actually meet and commit to trade.

a. Monopolistic competition
c. Human capital
b. Labour economics
d. Market structure

15. _____ has several particular meanings:

- in mathematics
    - _____ function
    - Euler _____
    - _____
    - _____ subgroup
    - method of _____s (partial differential equations)
- in physics and engineering
    - any _____ curve that shows the relationship between certain input- and output parameters, e.g.
    - an I-V or current-voltage _____ is the current in a circuit as a function of the applied voltage
    - Receiver-Operator _____
- in fiction
    - in Dungeons ' Dragons, _____ is another name for ability score

a. Russian financial crisis
c. Technocracy
b. Demand
d. Characteristic

16. An _____ is a market form in which a market or industry is dominated by a small number of sellers (oligopolists.) Because there are few participants in this type of market, each oligopolist is aware of the actions of the others. The decisions of one firm influence, and are influenced by, the decisions of other firms.

a. ACCRA Cost of Living Index
b. ACEA agreement
c. Oligopsony
d. Oligopoly

17. _____ in economics and business is the result of an exchange and from that trade we assign a numerical monetary value to a good, service or asset. If Alice trades Bob 4 apples for an orange, the _____ of an orange is 4 apples. Inversely, the _____ of an apple is 1/4 oranges.
   a. Premium pricing
   b. Price
   c. Price war
   d. Price book

18. A true _____ is a specific type of oligopoly where only two producers exist in one market. In reality, this definition is generally used where only two firms have dominant control over a market. In the field of industrial organization, it is the most commonly studied form of oligopoly due to its simplicity.
   a. Duopoly
   b. Megacorpstate
   c. 100-year flood
   d. 130-30 fund

19. In game theory, _____ is a solution concept of a game involving two or more players, in which each player is assumed to know the equilibrium strategies of the other players, and no player has anything to gain by changing only his or her own strategy unilaterally. If each player has chosen a strategy and no player can benefit by changing his or her strategy while the other players keep theirs unchanged, then the current set of strategy choices and the corresponding payoffs constitute a _____.

Stated simply, Amy and Bill are in _____ if Amy is making the best decision she can, taking into account Bill's decision, and Bill is making the best decision he can, taking into account Amy's decision.

   a. Linear production game
   b. Nash equilibrium
   c. Lump of labour
   d. Proper equilibrium

20. _____ is an agreement, usually secretive, which occurs between two or more persons to deceive, mislead or to obtain an objective forbidden by law typically involving fraud or gaining an unfair advantage. It is an agreement among firms to divide the market, set prices kickbacks, or misrepresenting the independence of the relationship between the colluding parties.' All acts effected by _____ are considered void.
   a. Dividing territories
   b. Net Book Agreement
   c. Bid rigging
   d. Collusion

21. In economics and sociology, an _____ is any factor (financial or non-financial) that enables or motivates a particular course of action, or counts as a reason for preferring one choice to the alternatives. It is an expectation that encourages people to behave in a certain way. Since human beings are purposeful creatures, the study of _____ structures is central to the study of all economic activity (both in terms of individual decision-making and in terms of co-operation and competition within a larger institutional structure.)
   a. Economic reform
   b. Epstein-Zin preferences
   c. Isocost
   d. Incentive

22. In game theory, a _____ is an extensive form game which consists in some number of repetitions of some base game (called a stage game.) The stage game is usually one of the well-studied 2-person games. It captures the idea that a player will have to take into account the impact of his current action on the future actions of other players; this is sometimes called his reputation.

a. Repeated Game
b. Correlated equilibrium
c. Pursuit-evasion
d. Quasi-perfect equilibrium

23. _____ was a survey conducted by the U.S. Department of Justice to gauge the prevalence of alcohol and illegal drug use among prior arrestees. It was a reformulation of the prior Drug Use Forecasting (DUF) program, focused on five drugs in particular: cocaine, marijuana, methamphetamine, opiates, and PCP.

Participants were randomly selected from arrest records in major metropolitan areas; because no personally identifying information is taken from each record chosen, the resulting data can be correlated to arrest rates, but not to the total population of persons charged.

a. ACEA agreement
b. ACCRA Cost of Living Index
c. AD-IA Model
d. Arrestee Drug Abuse Monitoring

24. Competition law, known in the United States as _____ law, has three main elements:

- prohibiting agreements or practices that restrict free trading and competition between business entities. This includes in particular the repression of cartels.
- banning abusive behaviour by a firm dominating a market, or anti-competitive practices that tend to lead to such a dominant position. Practices controlled in this way may include predatory pricing, tying, price gouging, refusal to deal, and many others.
- supervising the mergers and acquisitions of large corporations, including some joint ventures. Transactions that are considered to threaten the competitive process can be prohibited altogether, or approved subject to 'remedies' such as an obligation to divest part of the merged business or to offer licences or access to facilities to enable other businesses to continue competing.

The substance and practice of competition law varies from jurisdiction to jurisdiction. Protecting the interests of consumers (consumer welfare) and ensuring that entrepreneurs have an opportunity to compete in the market economy are often treated as important objectives. Competition law is closely connected with law on deregulation of access to markets, state aids and subsidies, the privatisation of state owned assets and the establishment of independent sector regulators. In recent decades, competition law has been viewed as a way to provide better public services.

a. Antitrust
b. Anti-Inflation Act
c. Intellectual property law
d. United Kingdom competition law

Chapter 13. Oligopoly and Monopolistic Competition

25. _____, known in the United States as antitrust law, has three main elements:

- prohibiting agreements or practices that restrict free trading and competition between business entities. This includes in particular the repression of cartels.
- banning abusive behaviour by a firm dominating a market, or anti-competitive practices that tend to lead to such a dominant position. Practices controlled in this way may include predatory pricing, tying, price gouging, refusal to deal, and many others.
- supervising the mergers and acquisitions of large corporations, including some joint ventures. Transactions that are considered to threaten the competitive process can be prohibited altogether, or approved subject to 'remedies' such as an obligation to divest part of the merged business or to offer licences or access to facilities to enable other businesses to continue competing.

The substance and practice of _____ varies from jurisdiction to jurisdiction. Protecting the interests of consumers (consumer welfare) and ensuring that entrepreneurs have an opportunity to compete in the market economy are often treated as important objectives. _____ is closely connected with law on deregulation of access to markets, state aids and subsidies, the privatisation of state owned assets and the establishment of independent sector regulators. In recent decades, _____ has been viewed as a way to provide better public services.

- a. Fee simple
- b. Hostile work environment
- c. Competition law
- d. Due diligence

26. The _____ is an independent agency of the United States government, established in 1914 by the _____ Act. Its principal mission is the promotion of 'consumer protection' and the elimination and prevention of what regulators perceive to be harmfully 'anti-competitive' business practices, such as coercive monopoly.

The _____ Act was one of President Wilson's major acts against trusts.

- a. Federal Trade Commission
- b. 1921 recession
- c. 100-year flood
- d. 130-30 fund

27. The _____ of 1914 (15 U.S.C §§ 41-58, as amended) established the Federal Trade Commission (FTC), a bipartisan body of five members appointed by the President of the United States for seven year terms. This Commission was authorized to issue Cease and Desist orders to large corporations to curb unfair trade practices. This Act also gave more flexibility to the US congress for judicial matters.

- a. Minimum wage law
- b. Competition law theory
- c. Buydown
- d. Federal Trade Commission Act

28.

The _____ was the first United States Federal statute to limit cartels and monopolies. It falls under antitrust law.

Chapter 13. Oligopoly and Monopolistic Competition

The Act provides: 'Every contract, combination in the form of trust or otherwise, or conspiracy, in restraint of trade or commerce among the several States, or with foreign nations, is declared to be illegal'. The Act also provides: 'Every person who shall monopolize, or attempt to monopolize, or combine or conspire with any other person or persons, to monopolize any part of the trade or commerce among the several States, or with foreign nations, shall be deemed guilty of a felony [. . .]' The Act put responsibility upon government attorneys and district courts to pursue and investigate trusts, companies and organizations suspected of violating the Act. The Clayton Act extended the right to sue under the antitrust laws to 'any person who shall be injured in his business or property by reason of anything forbidden in the antitrust laws.' Under the Clayton Act, private parties may sue in U.S. district court and should they prevail, they may be awarded treble damages and the cost of suit, including reasonable attorney's fees.

a. 100-year flood
b. 130-30 fund
c. Sherman Antitrust Act
d. 1921 recession

29. _____ was a Scottish moral philosopher and a pioneer of political economy. One of the key figures of the Scottish Enlightenment, Smith is the author of The Theory of Moral Sentiments and An Inquiry into the Nature and Causes of the Wealth of Nations. The latter, usually abbreviated as The Wealth of Nations, is considered his magnum opus and the first modern work of economics.

a. Adolf Hitler
b. Adolph Fischer
c. Alan Greenspan
d. Adam Smith

30. The _____ describes a firm's market power. It is defined by:

$$L = \frac{P - MC}{P}$$

where P is the market price set by the firm and MC is the firm's marginal cost. The index ranges from a high of 1 to a low of 0, with higher numbers implying greater market power.

a. Discounts and allowances
b. Break even analysis
c. Two-part tariff
d. Lerner Index

31. In economics, _____ is the process by which a firm determines the price and output level that returns the greatest profit. There are several approaches to this problem. The total revenue--total cost method relies on the fact that profit equals revenue minus cost, and the marginal revenue--marginal cost method is based on the fact that total profit in a perfectly competitive market reaches its maximum point where marginal revenue equals marginal cost.

a. Normal profit
b. 100-year flood
c. Profit margin
d. Profit maximization

32. In economics, _____ is equal to total cost divided by the number of goods produced (the output quantity, Q.) It is also equal to the sum of average variable costs (total variable costs divided by Q) plus average fixed costs (total fixed costs divided by Q.) _____s may be dependent on the time period considered (increasing production may be expensive or impossible in the short term, for example.)

a. Average variable cost
c. Explicit cost
b. Average cost
d. Average fixed cost

33. In economics, a _____ is a graph of the costs of production as a function of total quantity produced. In a free market economy, productively efficient firms use these curves to find the optimal point of production, where they make the most profits. There are a few different types of _____s, each relevant to a different area of economics.
   a. Demand curve
   c. Cost curve
   b. Kuznets curve
   d. Phillips curve

34. In microeconomics, _____ is quite simply the conversion of inputs into outputs. It is an economic process that uses resources to create a good or service that is suitable for exchange. This can include manufacturing, storing, shipping, and packaging.
   a. MET
   c. Red Guards
   b. Solved
   d. Production

35. An _____ is a tax levied on the financial income of people, corporations, or other legal entities. Various _____ systems exist, with varying degrees of tax incidence. Income taxation can be progressive, proportional, or regressive.
   a. AD-IA Model
   c. ACEA agreement
   b. ACCRA Cost of Living Index
   d. Income tax

36. A _____ is a consumption tax charged at the point of purchase for certain goods and services. The tax is usually set as a percentage by the government charging the tax. There is usually a list of exemptions.
   a. 1921 recession
   c. 130-30 fund
   b. 100-year flood
   d. Sales tax

37. To _____ is to impose a financial charge or other levy upon a taxpayer by a state or the functional equivalent of a state.

   _____es are also imposed by many subnational entities. _____es consist of direct _____ or indirect _____, and may be paid in money or as its labour equivalent (often but not always unpaid.)

   a. 130-30 fund
   c. 1921 recession
   b. Tax
   d. 100-year flood

38. To tax is to impose a financial charge or other levy upon a taxpayer by a state or the functional equivalent of a state.

   _____ are also imposed by many subnational entities. _____ consist of direct tax or indirect tax, and may be paid in money or as its labour equivalent (often but not always unpaid.)

   a. 130-30 fund
   c. Taxes
   b. 100-year flood
   d. 1921 recession

Chapter 13. Oligopoly and Monopolistic Competition

39. In economics, a common-pool resource, alternatively termed a _____ resource, is a particular type of good consisting of a natural or human-made resource system, the size or characteristics of which makes it costly, but not impossible, to exclude potential beneficiaries from obtaining benefits from its use. Unlike pure public goods, common pool resources face problems of congestion or overuse, because they are subtractable. A common-pool resource typically consists of a core resource, which defines the stock variable, while providing a limited quantity of extractable fringe units, which defines the flow variable.

   a. Common-pool resource
   b. Price-cap regulation
   c. Common property
   d. Government monopoly

40. A _____ is a duty imposed on goods when they are moved across a political boundary. They are usually associated with protectionism, the economic policy of restraining trade between nations. For political reasons, _____s are usually imposed on imported goods, although they may also be imposed on exported goods.

   a. 100-year flood
   b. 1921 recession
   c. 130-30 fund
   d. Tariff

41. In economics, an _____ is any good or commodity, transported from one country to another country in a legitimate fashion, typically for use in trade. _____ goods or services are provided to foreign consumers by domestic producers. _____ is an important part of international trade.

   a. ACCRA Cost of Living Index
   b. ACEA agreement
   c. AD-IA Model
   d. Export

42. The phrase _____ and acquisitions refers to the aspect of corporate strategy, corporate finance and management dealing with the buying, selling and combining of different companies that can aid, finance, or help a growing company in a given industry grow rapidly without having to create another business entity.

   An acquisition, also known as a takeover or a buyout, is the buying of one company (the 'target') by another. An acquisition may be friendly or hostile.

   a. Political economy
   b. Peace dividend
   c. Mergers
   d. Differential accumulation

43. The _____ is an important selective, mainly private, international organization designed by its founders to supervise and liberalize international trade. The organization officially commenced on 1 January 1995, under the Marrakesh Agreement, succeeding the 1947 General Agreement on Tariffs and Trade (GATT.)

   The _____ deals with regulation of trade between participating countries; it provides a framework for negotiating and formalising trade agreements, and a dispute resolution process aimed at enforcing participants' adherence to _____ agreements which are signed by representatives of member governments and ratified by their parliaments.

   a. Backus-Kehoe-Kydland consumption correlation puzzle
   b. 2009 G-20 London summit protests
   c. Bio-energy village
   d. World Trade Organization

Chapter 13. Oligopoly and Monopolistic Competition

44. In finance, a _____ is a debt security, in which the authorized issuer owes the holders a debt and, depending on the terms of the _____, is obliged to pay interest (the coupon) and/or to repay the principal at a later date, termed maturity. A _____ is a formal contract to repay borrowed money with interest at fixed intervals.

Thus a _____ is like a loan: the issuer is the borrower (debtor), the holder is the lender (creditor), and the coupon is the interest.

a. Callable
c. Zero-coupon
b. Prize Bond
d. Bond

45. Economics:

- _____, the desire to own something and the ability to pay for it
- _____ curve, a graphic representation of a _____ schedule
- _____ deposit, the money in checking accounts
- _____ pull theory, the theory that inflation occurs when _____ for goods and services exceeds existing supplies
- _____ schedule, a table that lists the quantity of a good a person will buy it each different price
- _____ side economics, the school of economics at believes government spending and tax cuts open economy by raising _____

a. McKesson ' Robbins scandal
c. Variability
b. Demand
d. Production

46. In economics, the _____ can be defined as the graph depicting the relationship between the price of a certain commodity, and the amount of it that consumers are willing and able to purchase at that given price. It is a graphic representation of a demand schedule. The _____ for all consumers together follows from the _____ of every individual consumer: the individual demands at each price are added together.

a. Kuznets curve
c. Cost curve
b. Wage curve
d. Demand curve

47. In economics, _____ is the ratio of the percent change in one variable to the percent change in another variable. It is a tool for measuring the responsiveness of a function to changes in parameters in a relative way. Commonly analyzed are _____ of substitution, price and wealth.

a. ACCRA Cost of Living Index
c. ACEA agreement
b. Elasticity
d. Elasticity of demand

48. In combinatorial game theory, a _____ is a directed graph whose nodes are positions in a game and whose edges are moves. The complete _____ for a game is the _____ starting at the initial position and containing all possible moves from each position. The first two ply of the _____ for tic-tac-toe.

The diagram shows the first two levels, or ply, in the _____ for tic-tac-toe.

a. Map-coloring games
b. Game complexity
c. Fuzzy game
d. Game tree

49. A _____ is a probabilistic model for which a graph denotes the conditional independence structure between random variables. They are commonly used in probability theory, statistics--particularly Bayesian statistics--and machine learning.

If the network structure of the model is a directed acyclic graph, the model represents a factorization of the joint probability of all random variables.

a. Marginal likelihood
b. Markov blanket
c. Density function
d. Graphical model

50. The Court of Justice of the European Communities, usually called the _____, is the highest court in the European Union in matters of European Community law. It has the ultimate say on matters of EU law in order to ensure its equal application across all EU member states.

The court was established in 1952 and is -- unlike most other Union institutions -- based in Luxembourg.

a. ACEA agreement
b. European Union
c. ACCRA Cost of Living Index
d. European Court of Justice

51. The _____ is an economic and political union of 27 member states, located primarily in Europe. It was established by the Treaty of Maastricht on 1 November 1993, upon the foundations of the pre-existing European Economic Community. With a population of almost 500 million, the _____ generates an estimated 30% share (US$18.4 trillion in 2008) of the nominal gross world product.

a. ACEA agreement
b. European Court of Justice
c. ACCRA Cost of Living Index
d. European Union

52. In economics, a _____ is a loss of economic efficiency that can occur when equilibrium for a good or service is not Pareto optimal. In other words, either people who would have more marginal benefit than marginal cost are not buying the good or service, or people who would have more marginal cost than marginal benefit are buying the product.

Causes of _____ can include monopoly pricing, externalities, taxes or subsidies, and binding price ceilings or floors.

a. Deadweight loss
b. Distributive efficiency
c. Leapfrogging
d. Contract curve

53. In economics, _____ are business expenses that are not dependent on the activities of the business They tend to be time-related, such as salaries or rents being paid per month. This is in contrast to variable costs, which are volume-related (and are paid per quantity.)

In management accounting, _____ are defined as expenses that do not change in proportion to the activity of a business, within the relevant period or scale of production.

a. Cost of poor quality
b. Quality costs
c. Fixed costs
d. Cost-Volume-Profit Analysis

54. In marketing, _____ is the process of distinguishing the differences of a product or offering from others, to make it more attractive to a particular target market. This involves differentiating it from competitors' products as well as one's own product offerings.

Differentiation is a source of competitive advantage.

a. Market segment
b. Pricing science
c. Technology acceptance model
d. Product differentiation

55. _____ exists when sales of identical goods or services are transacted at different prices from the same provider. In a theoretical market with perfect information, no transaction costs or prohibition on secondary exchange (or re-selling) to prevent arbitrage, _____ can only be a feature of monopoly and oligopoly markets, where market power can be exercised. Otherwise, the moment the seller tries to sell the same good at different prices, the buyer at the lower price can arbitrage by selling to the consumer buying at the higher price but with a tiny discount.

a. Lerner Index
b. Transfer pricing
c. Price discrimination
d. Loss leader

Chapter 14. Strategy

1. A _____ rocket is a rocket that uses two or more stages, each of which contains its own engines and propellant. A tandem or serial stage is mounted on top of another stage; a parallel stage is attached alongside another stage. The result is effectively two or more rockets stacked on top of or attached next to each other.
   - a. 100-year flood
   - b. 1921 recession
   - c. 130-30 fund
   - d. Multistage

2. _____ is an offer (often competitive) of setting a price one is willing to pay for something. A price offer is called a bid. The term may be used in context of auctions, stock exchange, card games, or real estate transactions.
   - a. Bord halfpenny
   - b. Normal good
   - c. Central limit order book
   - d. Bidding

3. In game theory, _____ is a solution concept of a game involving two or more players, in which each player is assumed to know the equilibrium strategies of the other players, and no player has anything to gain by changing only his or her own strategy unilaterally. If each player has chosen a strategy and no player can benefit by changing his or her strategy while the other players keep theirs unchanged, then the current set of strategy choices and the corresponding payoffs constitute a _____.

   Stated simply, Amy and Bill are in _____ if Amy is making the best decision she can, taking into account Bill's decision, and Bill is making the best decision he can, taking into account Amy's decision.

   - a. Linear production game
   - b. Proper equilibrium
   - c. Nash equilibrium
   - d. Lump of labour

4. A _____ is a counterfeit agreement among industries. It is an informal organization of producers that agree to coordinate prices and production. _____s usually occur in an oligopolistic industry, where there is a small number of sellers and usually involve homogeneous products.
   - a. Cartel
   - b. Shanzhai
   - c. Shill
   - d. 100-year flood

5. _____ is the transition of a national economy from monopoly control by groups of large businesses to a free market economy. This change rarely arises naturally, and is generally the result of regulation by a governing body.

   A modern example of _____ is the economic restructuring of Germany after the fall of the Third Reich in 1945.

   - a. Monopolization
   - b. Decartelization
   - c. Complementary monopoly
   - d. Market power

6. In economics, _____ are business expenses that are not dependent on the activities of the business They tend to be time-related, such as salaries or rents being paid per month. This is in contrast to variable costs, which are volume-related (and are paid per quantity.)

   In management accounting, _____ are defined as expenses that do not change in proportion to the activity of a business, within the relevant period or scale of production.

a. Fixed costs
c. Cost-Volume-Profit Analysis
b. Cost of poor quality
d. Quality costs

7. A _____ is the transfer of wealth from one party (such as a person or company) to another. A _____ is usually made in exchange for the provision of goods, services or both, or to fulfill a legal obligation.

The simplest and oldest form of _____ is barter, the exchange of one good or service for another.

a. Social gravity
c. Soft count
b. Going concern
d. Payment

8. Economics:

- _____, the desire to own something and the ability to pay for it
- _____ curve, a graphic representation of a _____ schedule
- _____ deposit, the money in checking accounts
- _____ pull theory, the theory that inflation occurs when _____ for goods and services exceeds existing supplies
- _____ schedule, a table that lists the quantity of a good a person will buy it each different price
- _____ side economics, the school of economics at believes government spending and tax cuts open economy by raising _____

a. McKesson ' Robbins scandal
c. Variability
b. Production
d. Demand

9. The _____ is an independent agency of the United States government, established in 1914 by the _____ Act. Its principal mission is the promotion of 'consumer protection' and the elimination and prevention of what regulators perceive to be harmfully 'anti-competitive' business practices, such as coercive monopoly.

The _____ Act was one of President Wilson's major acts against trusts.

a. 130-30 fund
c. 1921 recession
b. Federal Trade Commission
d. 100-year flood

10. A non-_____ is a term used in game theory economics to describe a threat by a player known to be rational in a sequential game that he would not carry out as it would not be in his best interest to do so. In game theoretical analysis the threat does not need to be a literally outspoken.

A simple example could be given by a person A walking up to another person B with a bomb.

a. Commodity fetishism
c. Debt to Assets
b. Black-Scholes
d. Credible threat

Chapter 14. Strategy

11. In combinatorial game theory, a _____ is a directed graph whose nodes are positions in a game and whose edges are moves. The complete _____ for a game is the _____ starting at the initial position and containing all possible moves from each position. The first two ply of the _____ for tic-tac-toe.

The diagram shows the first two levels, or ply, in the _____ for tic-tac-toe.

a. Fuzzy game
b. Map-coloring games
c. Game tree
d. Game complexity

12. In economics and finance, _____ is the change in total cost that arises when the quantity produced changes by one unit. It is the cost of producing one more unit of a good. Mathematically, the _____ function is expressed as the first derivative of the total cost (TC) function with respect to quantity (Q.)

a. Marginal cost
b. Variable cost
c. Khozraschyot
d. Quality costs

13. In economics, and cost accounting, _____ describes the total economic cost of production and is made up of variable costs, which vary according to the quantity of a good produced and include inputs such as labor and raw materials, plus fixed costs, which are independent of the quantity of a good produced and include inputs (capital) that cannot be varied in the short term, such as buildings and machinery. _____ in economics includes the total opportunity cost of each factor of production in addition to fixed and variable costs.

The rate at which _____ changes as the amount produced changes is called marginal cost.

a. 130-30 fund
b. Total cost
c. 1921 recession
d. 100-year flood

14. _____ refers to when a retailer or wholesaler is e;tiede; to purchase from a supplier on the understanding that no other distributor will be appointed or receive supplies in a given area. When the sales outlets are owned by the supplier, _____ is because of vertical integration, where the outlets are independent _____ is illegal due to the Restrictive Trade Practices Act, however, if it is registered and approved it is allowed.

_____ can be a barrier to entry.

a. ACEA agreement
b. AD-IA Model
c. ACCRA Cost of Living Index
d. Exclusive dealing

15. _____ are conceptually similar to economies of scale. Whereas economies of scale primarily refer to efficiencies associated with supply-side changes, such as increasing or decreasing the scale of production, of a single product type, _____ refer to efficiencies primarily associated with demand-side changes, such as increasing or decreasing the scope of marketing and distribution, of different types of products. _____ are one of the main reasons for such marketing strategies as product bundling, product lining, and family branding.

a. Economies of scale
b. Isoquant
c. Economic production quantity
d. Economies of scope

16. The _____ consists of a number of economic theories which describe the nature of the firm, company including its existence, its behaviour, and its relationship with the market.

In simplified terms, the _____ aims to answer these questions:

1. Existence - why do firms emerge, why are not all transactions in the economy mediated over the market?
2. Boundaries - why the boundary between firms and the market is located exactly there? Which transactions are performed internally and which are negotiated on the market?
3. Organization - why are firms structured in such specific way? What is the interplay of formal and informal relationships?

Despite looking simple, these questions are not answered by the established economic theory, which usually views firms as given, and treats them as black boxes without any internal structure.

The First World War period saw a change of emphasis in economic theory away from industry-level analysis which mainly included analysing markets to analysis at the level of the firm, as it became increasingly clear that perfect competition was no longer an adequate model of how firms behaved. Economic theory till then had focussed on trying to understand markets alone and there had been little study on understanding why firms or organisations exist.

a. Khazzoom-Brookes postulate
b. Policy Ineffectiveness Proposition
c. Technology gap
d. Theory of the firm

17. The Court of Justice of the European Communities, usually called the _____, is the highest court in the European Union in matters of European Community law. It has the ultimate say on matters of EU law in order to ensure its equal application across all EU member states.

The court was established in 1952 and is -- unlike most other Union institutions -- based in Luxembourg.

a. ACEA agreement
b. European Union
c. European Court of Justice
d. ACCRA Cost of Living Index

18. The _____ is an economic and political union of 27 member states, located primarily in Europe. It was established by the Treaty of Maastricht on 1 November 1993, upon the foundations of the pre-existing European Economic Community. With a population of almost 500 million, the _____ generates an estimated 30% share (US$18.4 trillion in 2008) of the nominal gross world product.

a. ACCRA Cost of Living Index
b. ACEA agreement
c. European Union
d. European Court of Justice

19. _____ is the advantage gained by the initial occupant of a market segment. This advantage may stem from the fact that the first entrant can gain control of resources that followers may not be able to match. Sometimes the first mover is not able to capitalise on its advantage, leaving the opportunity for another firm to gain second-mover advantage.

a. Continuous Improvement Process
b. Cross-docking
c. Business engineering
d. First-mover advantage

Chapter 14. Strategy

20. In economics, a _____ exists when a specific individual or enterprise has sufficient control over a particular product or service to determine significantly the terms on which other individuals shall have access to it. Monopolies are thus characterized by a lack of economic competition for the good or service that they provide and a lack of viable substitute goods. The verb 'monopolize' refers to the process by which a firm gains persistently greater market share than what is expected under perfect competition.

    a. 100-year flood   b. 1921 recession
    c. Monopoly   d. 130-30 fund

21. A _____ is a type of auction where the auctioneer begins with a high asking price which is lowered until some participant is willing to accept the auctioneer's price, or a predetermined reserve price (the seller's minimum acceptable price) is reached. The winning participant pays the last announced price. This is also known as a 'clock auction' or an open-outcry descending-price auction.

    a. Box social   b. French auction
    c. Vickrey auction   d. Dutch auction

22. _____ is a specific term used in companies' financial reporting from the company-whole point of view. Because that use excludes the effects of changing ownership interest, an economic measure of _____ is necessary for financial analysis from the shareholders' point of view

_____ is defined by the Financial Accounting Standards Board, or FASB, as e;the change in equity [net assets] of a business enterprise during a period from transactions and other events and circumstances from nonowner sources. It includes all changes in equity during a period except those resulting from investments by owners and distributions to owners.e;

_____ is the sum of net income and other items that must bypass the income statement because they have not been realized, including items like an unrealized holding gain or loss from available for sale securities and foreign currency translation gains or losses.

    a. Windfall gain   b. Real income
    c. Net national income   d. Comprehensive income

23. An _____ is a type of auction, whose most typical form is the 'open outcry' auction. The auctioneer opens the auction by announcing a Suggested Opening Bid, a starting price or reserve for the item on sale and then accepts increasingly higher bids from the floor consisting of buyers with a possible interest in the item. Unlike sealed bid auctions, 'open outcry' auctions are 'open' or fully transparent as the identity of all bidders is disclosed to each other bidder during the auction.

    a. Auction school   b. English auction
    c. Auction sniping   d. Online auction business model

24. _____ is the a method of technical and economic research of the systems for purpose to optimize a parity between system's consumer functions or properties and expenses to achieve those functions or properties.

This methodology for continuous perfection of production, industrial technologies, organizational structures was developed by Juryj Sobolev in 1948 at the 'Perm telephone factory'

- 1948 Juryj Sobolev - the first success in application of a method analysis at the 'Perm telephone factory'.
- 1949 - the first application for the invention as result of use of the new method.

Today in economically developed countries practically each enterprise or the company use methodology of the kind of functional-cost analysis as a practice of the quality management, most full satisfying to principles of standards of series ISO 9000.

- Interest of consumer not in products itself, but the advantage which it will receive from its usage.
- The consumer aspires to reduce his expenses
- Functions needed by consumer can be executed in the various ways, and, hence, with various efficiency and expenses. Among possible alternatives of realization of functions exist such in which the parity of quality and the price is the optimal for the consumer.

The goal of _____ is achievement of the highest consumer satisfaction of production at simultaneous decrease in all kinds of industrial expenses Classical _____ has three English synonyms - Value Engineering, Value Management, Value Analysis.

 a. Monopoly wage   b. Staple financing
 c. Willingness to pay   d. Function cost analysis

25. The _____ business model is a business model where a customer must pay a _____ price to have access to the product/service. The model was pioneered by magazines and newspapers, but is now used by many businesses and websites. Rather than selling products individually, a _____ sells periodic (monthly or yearly or seasonal) use or access to a product or service, or, in the case of such non-profit organizations as opera companies or symphony orchestras, it sells tickets to the entire run of five to fifteen scheduled performances for an entire season.
 a. Coopetition   b. Subscription
 c. Freebie marketing   d. Yield management

Chapter 15. Factor Markets and Vertical Integration

1. The _____ consists of a number of economic theories which describe the nature of the firm, company including its existence, its behaviour, and its relationship with the market.

In simplified terms, the _____ aims to answer these questions:

1. Existence - why do firms emerge, why are not all transactions in the economy mediated over the market?
2. Boundaries - why the boundary between firms and the market is located exactly there? Which transactions are performed internally and which are negotiated on the market?
3. Organization - why are firms structured in such specific way? What is the interplay of formal and informal relationships?

Despite looking simple, these questions are not answered by the established economic theory, which usually views firms as given, and treats them as black boxes without any internal structure.

The First World War period saw a change of emphasis in economic theory away from industry-level analysis which mainly included analysing markets to analysis at the level of the firm, as it became increasingly clear that perfect competition was no longer an adequate model of how firms behaved. Economic theory till then had focussed on trying to understand markets alone and there had been little study on understanding why firms or organisations exist.

   a. Policy Ineffectiveness Proposition
   c. Technology gap
   b. Khazzoom-Brookes postulate
   d. Theory of the firm

2. In economics, a _____ 'purchase') is a market form in which only one buyer faces many sellers. It is an example of imperfect competition, similar to a monopoly, in which only one seller faces many buyers. As the only purchaser of a good or service, the 'monopsonist' may dictate terms to its suppliers in the same manner that a monopolist controls the market for its buyers.
   a. Monopsony
   c. 100-year flood
   b. 1921 recession
   d. 130-30 fund

3. _____ in economics and business is the result of an exchange and from that trade we assign a numerical monetary value to a good, service or asset. If Alice trades Bob 4 apples for an orange, the _____ of an orange is 4 apples. Inversely, the _____ of an apple is 1/4 oranges.
   a. Price book
   c. Price war
   b. Premium pricing
   d. Price

4. _____ is the value of a coin, stamp or paper money, as printed on the coin, stamp or bill itself by the minting authority. While the _____ usually refers to the true value of the coin, stamp or bill in question (as with circulation coins) it can sometimes be largely symbolic, as is often the case with bullion coins. For example, a one troy ounce (31 g) American Gold Eagle bullion coin was worth and sold for about $670 USD during 2006 market prices (as of July 17, 2006) and yet has a _____ of only $50 USD.
   a. 130-30 fund
   c. Money Tracker
   b. 100-year flood
   d. Face value

5. In economics, the concept of the _____ refers to the decision-making time frame of a firm in which at least one factor of production is fixed. Costs which are fixed in the _____ have no impact on a firms decisions. For example a firm can raise output by increasing the amount of labour through overtime.

Chapter 15. Factor Markets and Vertical Integration

a. Hicks-neutral technical change
b. Product Pipeline
c. Short-run
d. Productivity model

6. _____ is an offer (often competitive) of setting a price one is willing to pay for something. A price offer is called a bid. The term may be used in context of auctions, stock exchange, card games, or real estate transactions.

a. Normal good
b. Central limit order book
c. Bord halfpenny
d. Bidding

7. In finance, a _____ is a debt security, in which the authorized issuer owes the holders a debt and, depending on the terms of the _____, is obliged to pay interest (the coupon) and/or to repay the principal at a later date, termed maturity. A _____ is a formal contract to repay borrowed money with interest at fixed intervals.

Thus a _____ is like a loan: the issuer is the borrower (debtor), the holder is the lender (creditor), and the coupon is the interest.

a. Zero-coupon
b. Callable
c. Prize Bond
d. Bond

8. Economics:

- _____,the desire to own something and the ability to pay for it
- _____ curve,a graphic representation of a _____ schedule
- _____ deposit, the money in checking accounts
- _____ pull theory,the theory that inflation occurs when _____ for goods and services exceeds existing supplies
- _____ schedule,a table that lists the quantity of a good a person will buy it each different price
- _____ side economics,the school of economics at believes government spending and tax cuts open economy by raising _____

a. Demand
b. McKesson ' Robbins scandal
c. Variability
d. Production

9. _____ is the a method of technical and economic research of the systems for purpose to optimize a parity between system's consumer functions or properties and expenses to achieve those functions or properties.

This methodology for continuous perfection of production, industrial technologies, organizational structures was developed by Juryj Sobolev in 1948 at the 'Perm telephone factory'

- 1948 Juryj Sobolev - the first success in application of a method analysis at the 'Perm telephone factory' .
- 1949 - the first application for the invention as result of use of the new method.

Chapter 15. Factor Markets and Vertical Integration

Today in economically developed countries practically each enterprise or the company use methodology of the kind of functional-cost analysis as a practice of the quality management, most full satisfying to principles of standards of series ISO 9000.

- Interest of consumer not in products itself, but the advantage which it will receive from its usage.
- The consumer aspires to reduce his expenses
- Functions needed by consumer can be executed in the various ways, and, hence, with various efficiency and expenses. Among possible alternatives of realization of functions exist such in which the parity of quality and the price is the optimal for the consumer.

The goal of _____ is achievement of the highest consumer satisfaction of production at simultaneous decrease in all kinds of industrial expenses Classical _____ has three English synonyms - Value Engineering, Value Management, Value Analysis.

a. Monopoly wage
b. Staple financing
c. Willingness to pay
d. Function cost analysis

10. In economics, the _____ or marginal physical product is the extra output produced by one more unit of an input (for instance, the difference in output when a firm's labour is increased from five to six units.) Assuming that no other inputs to production change, the _____ of a given input (X) can be expressed as:

_____ = $\Delta Y/\Delta X$ = (the change of Y)/(the change of X.)

-
  -
    - Pending approval by Thomas Sowell***

In neoclassical economics, this is the mathematical derivative of the production function.... Note that the 'product' (Y) is typically defined ignoring external costs and benefits.

a. Labor problem
b. Productive capacity
c. Factor prices
d. Marginal product

11. In economics, the _____ also known as MPL or MPN is the change in output from hiring one additional unit of labor. It is the increase in output added by the last unit of labor. Assuming that no other inputs to production change, the marginal product of a given input (X) can be expressed as:

MP = $\Delta Y/\Delta X$ = (the change of Y)/(the change of X.)

a. Marginal product
b. Marginal product of labor
c. Production function
d. Product Pipeline

12. In microeconomics, _____ is the extra revenue that an additional unit of product will bring. It is the additional income from selling one more unit of a good; sometimes equal to price. It can also be described as the change in total revenue/change in number of units sold.
   a. Market demand schedule
   b. Long term
   c. Marginal revenue
   d. Reservation price

13. The marginal revenue productivity theory of wages, also referred to as the _____ of labor, is the change in total revenue earned by a firm that results from employing one more unit of labor. It is a neoclassical model that determines, under some conditions, the optimal number of workers to employ at an exogenously determined market wage rate.

The _____ of a worker is equal to the product of the marginal product of labor (MP) and the marginal revenue (MR), given by MR×MP = _____.

   a. Real prices and ideal prices
   b. Marginal revenue productivity theory of wages
   c. Coal depletion
   d. Marginal revenue product

14. In economics, _____ is the process by which a firm determines the price and output level that returns the greatest profit. There are several approaches to this problem. The total revenue--total cost method relies on the fact that profit equals revenue minus cost, and the marginal revenue--marginal cost method is based on the fact that total profit in a perfectly competitive market reaches its maximum point where marginal revenue equals marginal cost.
   a. 100-year flood
   b. Normal profit
   c. Profit maximization
   d. Profit margin

15. In microeconomics, _____ is quite simply the conversion of inputs into outputs. It is an economic process that uses resources to create a good or service that is suitable for exchange. This can include manufacturing, storing, shipping, and packaging.
   a. Production
   b. MET
   c. Red Guards
   d. Solved

16. _____ exists when sales of identical goods or services are transacted at different prices from the same provider. In a theoretical market with perfect information, no transaction costs or prohibition on secondary exchange (or re-selling) to prevent arbitrage, _____ can only be a feature of monopoly and oligopoly markets, where market power can be exercised. Otherwise, the moment the seller tries to sell the same good at different prices, the buyer at the lower price can arbitrage by selling to the consumer buying at the higher price but with a tiny discount.
   a. Price discrimination
   b. Lerner Index
   c. Transfer pricing
   d. Loss leader

17. In economics, the _____ functional form of production functions is widely used to represent the relationship of an output to inputs. It was proposed by Knut Wicksell (1851-1926), and tested against statistical evidence by Charles Cobb and Paul Douglas in 1900-1928.

For production, the function is

$$Y = AL^{\alpha}K^{\beta},$$

where:

- Y = total production (the monetary value of all goods produced in a year)
- L = labor input
- K = capital input
- A = total factor productivity
- α and β are the output elasticities of labor and capital, respectively. These values are constants determined by available technology.

Output elasticity measures the responsiveness of output to a change in levels of either labor or capital used in production, ceteris paribus. For example if α = 0.15, a 1% increase in labor would lead to approximately a 0.15% increase in output.

a. Growth accounting
b. Social savings
c. Demand-pull theory
d. Cobb-Douglas

18. In economics, the _____ can be defined as the graph depicting the relationship between the price of a certain commodity, and the amount of it that consumers are willing and able to purchase at that given price. It is a graphic representation of a demand schedule. The _____ for all consumers together follows from the _____ of every individual consumer: the individual demands at each price are added together.

a. Wage curve
b. Kuznets curve
c. Cost curve
d. Demand curve

19. In economics, a _____ is a function that specifies the output of a firm, an industry, or an entire economy for all combinations of inputs. A meta-_____ compares the practice of the existing entities converting inputs X into output y to determine the most efficient practice _____ of the existing entities, whether the most efficient feasible practice production or the most efficient actual practice production. In either case, the maximum output of a technologically-determined production process is a mathematical function of input factors of production.

a. Post-Fordism
b. Short-run
c. Constant elasticity of substitution
d. Production function

20. In economic models, the _____ time frame assumes no fixed factors of production. Firms can enter or leave the marketplace, and the cost (and availability) of land, labor, raw materials, and capital goods can be assumed to vary. In contrast, in the short-run time frame, certain factors are assumed to be fixed, because there is not sufficient time for them to change.

a. Productivity world
b. Long-run
c. Diseconomies of scale
d. Price/performance ratio

21. A true _____ is a specific type of oligopoly where only two producers exist in one market. In reality, this definition is generally used where only two firms have dominant control over a market. In the field of industrial organization, it is the most commonly studied form of oligopoly due to its simplicity.

a. Megacorpstate
b. 100-year flood
c. 130-30 fund
d. Duopoly

Chapter 15. Factor Markets and Vertical Integration

22. In economics, _____ describes the state of a market with respect to competition.

- Perfect competition, in which the market consists of a very large number of firms producing a homogeneous product.
- Monopolistic competition where there are a large number of independent firms which have a very small proportion of the market share.
- Oligopoly, in which a market is dominated by a small number of firms which own more than 40% of the market share.
- Oligopsony, a market dominated by many sellers and a few buyers.
- Monopoly, where there is only one provider of a product or service.
- Natural monopoly, a monopoly in which economies of scale cause efficiency to increase continuously with the size of the firm. A firm is a natural monopoly if it is able to serve the entire market demand at a lower cost than any combination of two or more smaller, more specialized firms.
- Monopsony, when there is only one buyer in a market.

The imperfectly competitive structure is quite identical to the realistic market conditions where some monopolistic competitors, monopolists, oligopolists, and duopolists exist and dominate the market conditions. The elements of _____ include the number and size distribution of firms, entry conditions, and the extent of differentiation.

These somewhat abstract concerns tend to determine some but not all details of a specific concrete market system where buyers and sellers actually meet and commit to trade.

a. Monopolistic competition
c. Market structure
b. Human capital
d. Labour economics

23. _____ has several particular meanings:

- in mathematics
    - _____ function
    - Euler _____
    - _____
    - _____ subgroup
    - method of _____ s (partial differential equations)
- in physics and engineering
    - any _____ curve that shows the relationship between certain input- and output parameters, e.g.
    - an I-V or current-voltage _____ is the current in a circuit as a function of the applied voltage
    - Receiver-Operator _____
- in fiction
    - in Dungeons ' Dragons, _____ is another name for ability score

a. Russian financial crisis
c. Technocracy
b. Demand
d. Characteristic

Chapter 15. Factor Markets and Vertical Integration

24. Competitive market equilibrium is the traditional concept of economic equilibrium, appropriate for the analysis of commodity markets with flexible prices and many traders, and serving as the benchmark of efficiency in economic analysis. It relies crucially on the assumption of a competitive environment where each trader decides upon a quantity that is so small compared to the total quantity traded in the market that their individual transactions have no influence on the prices. Competitive markets are an ideal, a standard that other market structures are evaluated by.

A _____ consists of a vector of prices and an allocation such that given the prices, each trader by maximizing his objective function (profit, preferences) subject to his technological possibilities and resource constraints plans to trade into his part of the proposed allocation, and such that the prices make all net trades compatible with one another ('clear the market') by equating aggregate supply and demand for the commodities which are traded.

- a. Partial equilibrium
- b. Competitive equilibrium
- c. Product-Market Growth Matrix
- d. Market system

25. _____ is the term denoting either an entrance or changes which are inserted into a system and which activate/modify a process. It is an abstract concept, used in the modeling, system(s) design and system(s) exploitation. It is usually connected with other terms, e.g., _____ field, _____ variable, _____ parameter, _____ value, _____ signal, _____ device and _____ file.

- a. AD-IA Model
- b. ACCRA Cost of Living Index
- c. ACEA agreement
- d. Input

26. In economics, _____ is the ability of a firm to alter the market price of a good or service. A firm with _____ can raise prices without losing all customers to competitors.

When a firm has _____ it faces a downward-sloping demand curve.

- a. Revenue-cap regulation
- b. Market power
- c. Pacman conjecture
- d. Price makers

27. A trade union or _____ is an organization of workers who have banded together to achieve common goals in key areas and working conditions. The trade union, through its leadership, bargains with the employer on behalf of union members (rank and file members) and negotiates labor contracts (Collective bargaining) with employers. This may include the negotiation of wages, work rules, complaint procedures, rules governing hiring, firing and promotion of workers, benefits, workplace safety and policies.

- a. Demand-side technologies
- b. Labor union
- c. Basis of futures
- d. Business valuation standards

28. A _____ or labor union is an organization of workers who have banded together to achieve common goals in key areas and working conditions. The _____, through its leadership, bargains with the employer on behalf of union members (rank and file members) and negotiates labor contracts (Collective bargaining) with employers. This may include the negotiation of wages, work rules, complaint procedures, rules governing hiring, firing and promotion of workers, benefits, workplace safety and policies.

- a. Case-Shiller Home Price Indices
- b. Guaranteed investment contracts
- c. Consumer goods
- d. Trade union

Chapter 15. Factor Markets and Vertical Integration

29. In economics, a _____ exists when a specific individual or enterprise has sufficient control over a particular product or service to determine significantly the terms on which other individuals shall have access to it. Monopolies are thus characterized by a lack of economic competition for the good or service that they provide and a lack of viable substitute goods. The verb 'monopolize' refers to the process by which a firm gains persistently greater market share than what is expected under perfect competition.
   a. 100-year flood
   c. 1921 recession
   b. 130-30 fund
   d. Monopoly

30. An _____ is a market form in which the number of buyers is small while the number of sellers in theory could be large. This typically happens in market for inputs where a small number of firms are competing to obtain factors of production. It contrasts with an oligopoly, where there are many buyers but just a few sellers.
   a. Oligopsony
   c. ACEA agreement
   b. Oligopoly
   d. ACCRA Cost of Living Index

31. To _____ is to impose a financial charge or other levy upon a taxpayer by a state or the functional equivalent of a state.

_____es are also imposed by many subnational entities. _____es consist of direct _____ or indirect _____, and may be paid in money or as its labour equivalent (often but not always unpaid.)

   a. Tax
   c. 1921 recession
   b. 130-30 fund
   d. 100-year flood

32. _____ or economic opportunity loss is the value of the next best alternative foregone as the result of making a decision. _____ analysis is an important part of a company's decision-making processes but is not treated as an actual cost in any financial statement. The next best thing that a person can engage in is referred to as the _____ of doing the best thing and ignoring the next best thing to be done.
   a. Economic ideology
   c. Opportunity cost
   b. Industrial organization
   d. Economic

33. In economics and related disciplines, a _____ is a cost incurred in making an economic exchange. For example, most people, when buying or selling a stock, must pay a commission to their broker; that commission is a _____ of doing the stock deal. Or consider buying a banana from a store; to purchase the banana, your costs will be not only the price of the banana itself, but also the energy and effort it requires to find out which of the various banana products you prefer, where to get them and at what price, the cost of traveling from your house to the store and back, the time waiting in line, and the effort of the paying itself; the costs above and beyond the cost of the banana are the _____s.
   a. Transaction cost
   c. Sliding scale fees
   b. Cost allocation
   d. Cost of poor quality

34. An _____ is a tax based on the value of real estate or personal property. It is more common than the opposite, a specific duty, or a tax based on the quantity of an item regardless of price.

An _____ is typically imposed at the time of a transaction), but it may be imposed on an annual basis (real or personal property tax) or in connection with another significant event (inheritance tax, surrendering citizenship, or tariffs).

Chapter 15. Factor Markets and Vertical Integration

a. User charge
b. Optimal tax
c. Indirect tax
d. Ad valorem tax

35. An _____ is a tax levied on the financial income of people, corporations, or other legal entities. Various _____ systems exist, with varying degrees of tax incidence. Income taxation can be progressive, proportional, or regressive.
   a. AD-IA Model
   b. ACCRA Cost of Living Index
   c. ACEA agreement
   d. Income tax

36. A _____ is a consumption tax charged at the point of purchase for certain goods and services. The tax is usually set as a percentage by the government charging the tax. There is usually a list of exemptions.
   a. 1921 recession
   b. 100-year flood
   c. 130-30 fund
   d. Sales tax

37. A _____ is a duty imposed on goods when they are moved across a political boundary. They are usually associated with protectionism, the economic policy of restraining trade between nations. For political reasons, _____s are usually imposed on imported goods, although they may also be imposed on exported goods.
   a. 1921 recession
   b. 100-year flood
   c. Tariff
   d. 130-30 fund

38. To tax is to impose a financial charge or other levy upon a taxpayer by a state or the functional equivalent of a state.

_____ are also imposed by many subnational entities. _____ consist of direct tax or indirect tax, and may be paid in money or as its labour equivalent (often but not always unpaid.)

   a. 130-30 fund
   b. 100-year flood
   c. 1921 recession
   d. Taxes

39. In economics, a common-pool resource, alternatively termed a _____ resource, is a particular type of good consisting of a natural or human-made resource system, the size or characteristics of which makes it costly, but not impossible, to exclude potential beneficiaries from obtaining benefits from its use. Unlike pure public goods, common pool resources face problems of congestion or overuse, because they are subtractable. A common-pool resource typically consists of a core resource, which defines the stock variable, while providing a limited quantity of extractable fringe units, which defines the flow variable.
   a. Government monopoly
   b. Price-cap regulation
   c. Common property
   d. Common-pool resource

40. A _____ refers to property being sold by a taxing authority or the court to recover delinquent taxes.

When property taxes are not paid, title gets transferred to the state. The owner will then have a period of time to redeem the property by paying the overdue taxes, including penalties and costs.

   a. Tax Sale
   b. Tax wedge
   c. Taxation as theft
   d. Tax competition

41. The _____ describes a firm's market power. It is defined by:

$$L = \frac{P - MC}{P}$$

where P is the market price set by the firm and MC is the firm's marginal cost. The index ranges from a high of 1 to a low of 0, with higher numbers implying greater market power.

a. Two-part tariff
b. Break even analysis
c. Discounts and allowances
d. Lerner Index

Chapter 16. Interest Rates, Investments, and Capital Markets

1. In Marxian economics, _____ originally referred to the means of production. Individuals, organizations and governments use _____ in the production of other goods or commodities. _____ include factories, machinery, tools, equipment, and various buildings which are used to produce other products for consumption.
    a. Capital deepening
    b. Wealth inequality in the United States
    c. Capital intensive
    d. Capital goods

2. In economics, a _____ or a hard good is a good which does not quickly wear out it yields services or utility over time rather than being completely used up when used once. Most goods are therefore _____s to a certain degree. These are goods that can last for a relatively long time, such as refrigerators, cars, and DVD players.
    a. Luxury good
    b. Superior goods
    c. Durable good
    d. Search good

3. A _____ is an object whose consumption increases the utility of the consumer, for which the quantity demanded exceeds the quantity supplied at zero price. _____s are usually modeled as having diminishing marginal utility. The first individual purchase has high utility; the second has less.
    a. Pie method
    b. Composite good
    c. Merit good
    d. Good

4. The _____ is the market for securities, where companies and governments can raise longterm funds. It is a market in which money is lent for periods longer than a year. The _____ includes the stock market and the bond market.
    a. Financial instrument
    b. Performance attribution
    c. Capital market
    d. Multi-family office

5. _____ is an online peer-reviewed magazine published by the Agricultural ' Applied Economics Association (AAEA) for readers interested in the policy and management of agriculture, the food industry, natural resources, rural communities, and the environment. _____ is published quarterly and is available free online. It is currently one of three outreach products offered by AAEA, along with the more timely Policy Issues and the forthcoming Shared Materials section of the AAEA Web site.
    a. Choices
    b. 100-year flood
    c. 1921 recession
    d. 130-30 fund

6. Economics:

    - _____, the desire to own something and the ability to pay for it
    - _____ curve, a graphic representation of a _____ schedule
    - _____ deposit, the money in checking accounts
    - _____ pull theory, the theory that inflation occurs when _____ for goods and services exceeds existing supplies
    - _____ schedule, a table that lists the quantity of a good a person will buy it each different price
    - _____ side economics, the school of economics at believes government spending and tax cuts open economy by raising _____

    a. Variability
    b. Demand
    c. McKesson ' Robbins scandal
    d. Production

Chapter 16. Interest Rates, Investments, and Capital Markets

7. Discounting is a financial mechanism in which a debtor obtains the right to delay payments to a creditor, for a defined period of time, in exchange for a charge or fee. Essentially, the party that owes money in the present purchases the right to delay the payment until some future date. The _____, or charge, is simply the difference between the original amount owed in the present and the amount that has to be paid in the future to settle the debt.
   a. Reliability theory
   b. Reinsurance
   c. Certified Risk Manager
   d. Discount

8. The _____ is an interest rate a central bank charges depository institutions that borrow reserves from it.

The term _____ has two meanings:

   - the same as interest rate; the term 'discount' does not refer to the meaning of the word, but to the purpose of using the quantity, such as computations of present value, e.g. net present value or discounted cash flow

   - the annual effective _____, which is the annual interest divided by the capital including that interest; this rate is lower than the interest rate; it corresponds to using the value after a year as the nominal value, and seeing the initial value as the nominal value minus a discount; it is used for Treasury Bills and similar financial instruments

The annual effective _____ is the annual interest divided by the capital including that interest, which is the interest rate divided by 100% plus the interest rate. It is the annual discount factor to be applied to the future cash flow, to find the discount, subtracted from a future value to find the value one year earlier.

For example, suppose there is a government bond that sells for $95 and pays $100 in a year's time.

   a. Stochastic volatility
   b. Discount rate
   c. Johansen test
   d. Perpetuity

9. _____ is a fee paid on borrowed assets. It is the price paid for the use of borrowed money, or, money earned by deposited funds. Assets that are sometimes lent with _____ include money, shares, consumer goods through hire purchase, major assets such as aircraft, and even entire factories in finance lease arrangements.
   a. Insolvency
   b. Internal debt
   c. Interest
   d. Asset protection

10. An _____ is the price a borrower pays for the use of money they do not own, for instance a small company might borrow from a bank to kick start their business, and the return a lender receives for deferring the use of funds, by lending it to the borrower. _____s are normally expressed as a percentage rate over the period of one year.

_____s targets are also a vital tool of monetary policy and are used to control variables like investment, inflation, and unemployment.

   a. Arrow-Debreu model
   b. Enterprise value
   c. Interest rate
   d. ACCRA Cost of Living Index

Chapter 16. Interest Rates, Investments, and Capital Markets

11. In finance, a _____ is a debt security, in which the authorized issuer owes the holders a debt and, depending on the terms of the _____, is obliged to pay interest (the coupon) and/or to repay the principal at a later date, termed maturity. A _____ is a formal contract to repay borrowed money with interest at fixed intervals.

Thus a _____ is like a loan: the issuer is the borrower (debtor), the holder is the lender (creditor), and the coupon is the interest.

   a. Callable
   c. Prize Bond
   b. Zero-coupon
   d. Bond

12. _____ in economics and business is the result of an exchange and from that trade we assign a numerical monetary value to a good, service or asset. If Alice trades Bob 4 apples for an orange, the _____ of an orange is 4 apples. Inversely, the _____ of an apple is 1/4 oranges.
   a. Price book
   c. Premium pricing
   b. Price war
   d. Price

13. In statistics the _____ of an event i is the number n_i of times the event occurred in the experiment or the study. These frequencies are often graphically represented in histograms.

We speak of absolute frequencies, when the counts n_i themselves are given and of (relative) frequencies, when those are normalized by the total number of events:

$$f_i = \frac{n_i}{N} = \frac{n_i}{\sum_i n_i}.$$

Taking the f_i for all i and tabulating or plotting them leads to a _____ distribution.

   a. Frequency
   c. 130-30 fund
   b. 100-year flood
   d. 1921 recession

14. The terms _____ , nominal _____, and effective _____ describe the interest rate for a whole year (annualized), rather than just a monthly fee/rate, as applied on a loan, mortgage, credit card, etc. It is a finance charge expressed as an annual rate. Those terms have formal, legal definitions in some countries or legal jurisdictions, but in general:

  • The nominal _____ is the simple-interest rate (for a year.)
  • The effective _____ is the fee+compound interest rate (calculated across a year.)

The nominal _____ is calculated as: the rate, for a payment period, multiplied by the number of payment periods in a year. However, the exact legal definition of 'effective _____', or EAR in short, can vary greatly in each jurisdiction, depending on the type of fees included, such as participation fees, loan origination fees, monthly service charges, or late fees. The effective _____ has been called the 'mathematically-true' interest rate for each year.

a. Annual percentage rate
b. Universal bank
c. Arranger
d. Automatic transfer service account

15. _____ measures the nominal future sum of money that a given sum of money is 'worth' at a specified time in the future assuming a certain interest rate rate of return; it is the present value multiplied by the accumulation function.

The value does not include corrections for inflation or other factors that affect the true value of money in the future. This is used in time value of money calculations.

a. Negative gearing
b. Present value
c. Future value
d. Future-oriented

16. _____ is the value on a given date of a future payment or series of future payments, discounted to reflect the time value of money and other factors such as investment risk. _____ calculations are widely used in business and economics to provide a means to compare cash flows at different times on a meaningful 'like to like' basis.

Money value fluctuates over time: $100 today are not worth $100 in five years.

a. Future value
b. Present value of costs
c. Present value
d. Tax shield

17. _____ is the a method of technical and economic research of the systems for purpose to optimize a parity between system's consumer functions or properties and expenses to achieve those functions or properties.

This methodology for continuous perfection of production, industrial technologies, organizational structures was developed by Juryj Sobolev in 1948 at the 'Perm telephone factory'

- 1948 Juryj Sobolev - the first success in application of a method analysis at the 'Perm telephone factory' .
- 1949 - the first application for the invention as result of use of the new method.

Today in economically developed countries practically each enterprise or the company use methodology of the kind of functional-cost analysis as a practice of the quality management, most full satisfying to principles of standards of series ISO 9000.

- Interest of consumer not in products itself, but the advantage which it will receive from its usage.
- The consumer aspires to reduce his expenses
- Functions needed by consumer can be executed in the various ways, and, hence, with various efficiency and expenses. Among possible alternatives of realization of functions exist such in which the parity of quality and the price is the optimal for the consumer.

The goal of _____ is achievement of the highest consumer satisfaction of production at simultaneous decrease in all kinds of industrial expenses Classical _____ has three English synonyms - Value Engineering, Value Management, Value Analysis.

Chapter 16. Interest Rates, Investments, and Capital Markets

a. Staple financing
c. Willingness to pay
b. Monopoly wage
d. Function cost analysis

18. A _____ is the transfer of wealth from one party (such as a person or company) to another. A _____ is usually made in exchange for the provision of goods, services or both, or to fulfill a legal obligation.

The simplest and oldest form of _____ is barter, the exchange of one good or service for another.

a. Going concern
c. Social gravity
b. Soft count
d. Payment

19. _____ is the point where a person stops employment completely. A person may also semi-retire and keep some sort of _____ job, out of choice rather than necessity. This usually happens upon reaching a determined age, when physical conditions don't allow the person to work any more (by illness or accident), or even for personal choice (usually in the presence of an adequate pension or personal savings.)

a. Termination of employment
c. Layoff
b. 100-year flood
d. Retirement

20. In economics, _____ is a rise in the general level of prices of goods and services in an economy over a period of time. When the general price level rises, each unit of currency buys fewer goods and services; consequently, _____ is also a decline in the real value of money--a loss of purchasing power in the medium of exchange which is also the monetary unit of account in the economy. A chief measure of general price-level _____ is the general _____ rate, which is the percentage change in a general price index (normally the Consumer Price Index) over time.

a. Economic
c. Energy economics
b. Opportunity cost
d. Inflation

21. _____ is the process of adjusting economic indicators and the prices of goods and services from different time periods to the same price level. To adjust for inflation, an indicator is divided by the inflation index.

It is easy to show that 7% inflation, lasting 10 years, would nearly double the cost of living (1.07^{10}=1.96.)

a. Investment goods
c. Inflation adjustment
b. Alternative employment arrangements
d. International Marketmakers Combination

22. The '_____' is approximately the nominal interest rate minus the inflation rate Since the inflation rate over the course of a loan is not known initially, volatility in inflation represents a risk to both the lender and the borrower.

In economics and finance, an individual who lends money for repayment at a later point in time expects to be compensated for the time value of money, or not having the use of that money while it is lent.

a. Core inflation
c. Real interest rate
b. Cost-push inflation
d. Reflation

Chapter 16. Interest Rates, Investments, and Capital Markets

23. _____ is a financial mechanism in which a debtor obtains the right to delay payments to a creditor, for a defined period of time, in exchange for a charge or fee. Essentially, the party that owes money in the present purchases the right to delay the payment until some future date. The discount, or charge, is simply the difference between the original amount owed in the present and the amount that has to be paid in the future to settle the debt.
    a. Certified Risk Manager   b. Discounting
    c. Maximum life span   d. Generalized linear model

24. In finance and economics _____ or nominal rate of interest refers to the rate of interest before adjustment for inflation (in contrast with the real interest rate); or, for interest rates 'as stated' without adjustment for the full effect of compounding (also referred to as the nominal annual rate.) An interest rate is called nominal if the frequency of compounding (e.g. a month) is not identical to the basic time unit (normally a year.)

The real interest rate includes compensation for the lender's lost value due to inflation, whereas the _____ excludes inflation.

    a. London Interbank Offered Rate   b. Risk-free interest rate
    c. Fixed interest   d. Nominal Interest rate

25. _____ or net present worth (NPW) is defined as the total present value (PV) of a time series of cash flows. It is a standard method for using the time value of money to appraise long-term projects. Used for capital budgeting, and widely throughout economics, it measures the excess or shortfall of cash flows, in present value terms, once financing charges are met.
    a. Maturity   b. Net present value
    c. Future value   d. Refinancing risk

Chapter 16. Interest Rates, Investments, and Capital Markets

26. A _____ is:

- Rewrite _____, in generative grammar and computer science
- Standardization, a formal and widely-accepted statement, fact, definition, or qualification
- Operation, a determinate _____ for performing a mathematical operation and obtaining a certain result (Mathematics, Logic)
    - Unary operation
    - Binary operation
- _____ of inference, a function from sets of formulae to formulae (Mathematics, Logic)
- _____ of thumb, principle with broad application that is not intended to be strictly accurate or reliable for every situation. Also often simply referred to as a _____
- Moral, an atomic element of a moral code for guiding choices in human behavior
- Heuristic, a quantized '_____' which shows a tendency or probability for successful function
- A regulation, as in sports
- A Production _____, as in computer science
- Procedural law, a _____ set governing the application of laws to cases
    - A law, which may informally be called a '_____'
    - A court ruling, a decision by a court
- In the U.S. Government, a regulation mandated by Congress, but written or expanded upon by the Executive Branch.
- Norm (sociology), an informal but widely accepted _____, concept, truth, definition, or qualification (social norms, legal norms, coding norms)
- Norm (philosophy), a kind of sentence or a reason to act, feel or believe
- 'Rulership' is the concept of governance by a government:
    - Military _____, governance by a military body
    - Monastic _____, a collection of precepts that guides the life of monks or nuns in a religious order where the superior holds the place of Christ
- Slide _____

- '_____,' a song by Ayumi Hamasaki
- '_____,' a song by rapper Nas
- '_____s,' an album by the band The Whitest Boy Alive
- _____s: Pyaar Ka Superhit Formula, a 2003 Bollywood film
- ruler, an instrument for measuring lengths
- _____, a component of an astrolabe, circumferator or similar instrument
- The _____s, a bestselling self-help book
- _____ Project (Run Up-to-date Linux Everywhere), a project that aims to use up-to-date Linux software on old PCs
- _____ engine, a software system that helps managing business _____s
- Ja _____, a hip hop artist
    - R.U.L.E., a 2005 greatest hits album by rapper Ja _____
- '_____s,' a KMFDM song

a. Demand
c. Rule
b. Procter ' Gamble
d. Technocracy

Chapter 16. Interest Rates, Investments, and Capital Markets

27. In finance, _____ rate of profit or sometimes just return, is the ratio of money gained or lost on an investment relative to the amount of money invested. The amount of money gained or lost may be referred to as interest, profit/loss, gain/loss, or net income/loss. The money invested may be referred to as the asset, capital, principal, or the cost basis of the investment.
    a. Sortino ratio
    b. Cost accrual ratio
    c. Current ratio
    d. Rate of return

28. _____ is the value of a coin, stamp or paper money, as printed on the coin, stamp or bill itself by the minting authority. While the _____ usually refers to the true value of the coin, stamp or bill in question (as with circulation coins) it can sometimes be largely symbolic, as is often the case with bullion coins. For example, a one troy ounce (31 g) American Gold Eagle bullion coin was worth and sold for about $670 USD during 2006 market prices (as of July 17, 2006) and yet has a _____ of only $50 USD.
    a. Face value
    b. Money Tracker
    c. 100-year flood
    d. 130-30 fund

29. _____ refers to the stock of skills and knowledge embodied in the ability to perform labor so as to produce economic value. It is the skills and knowledge gained by a worker through education and experience. Many early economic theories refer to it simply as labor, one of three factors of production, and consider it to be a fungible resource -- homogeneous and easily interchangeable. Other conceptions of labor dispense with these assumptions.
    a. Law of increasing costs
    b. Human capital
    c. Price theory
    d. General equilibrium

30. _____s is the social science that studies the production, distribution, and consumption of goods and services. The term _____s comes from the Ancient Greek oá¼°κονομῖα from oá¼¶κος (oikos, 'house') + vÏŒμος (nomos, 'custom' or 'law'), hence 'rules of the house(hold)'. Current _____ models developed out of the broader field of political economy in the late 19th century, owing to a desire to use an empirical approach more akin to the physical sciences.
    a. Opportunity cost
    b. Inflation
    c. Energy economics
    d. Economic

31. _____ and behavioral finance are closely related fields that have evolved to be a separate branch of economic and financial analysis which applies scientific research on human and social, cognitive and emotional factors to better understand economic decisions by consumers, borrowers, investors, and how they affect market prices, returns and the allocation of resources.

    The field is primarily concerned with the bounds of rationality (selfishness, self-control) of economic agents. Behavioral models typically integrate insights from psychology with neo-classical economic theory.

    a. Neoclassical economics
    b. Mainstream economics
    c. Behavioral economics
    d. Georgism

32. In economics, _____ is the active redirecting resources from being consumed today so that they may create benefits in the future; the use of assets to earn income or profit. _____ is the process of making an investment in order to earn a profit, for example equity investment either through a fund, a 401k plan, or individually. People often invest in order to build up their estate or to accumulate funds for retirement.

Chapter 16. Interest Rates, Investments, and Capital Markets

To try to predict good stocks to invest in, two main schools of thought exist: technical analysis and fundamentals analysis.

a. AD-IA Model
b. ACCRA Cost of Living Index
c. ACEA agreement
d. Investing

33. _____ is the increase in the average temperature of the Earth's near-surface air and oceans since the mid-twentieth century and its projected continuation. Global surface temperature increased 0.74 ± 0.18 °C (1.33 ± 0.32 °F) during the last century. The Intergovernmental Panel on Climate Change (IPCC) concludes that anthropogenic greenhouse gases are responsible for most of the observed temperature increase since the middle of the twentieth century, and that natural phenomena such as solar variation and volcanoes probably had a small warming effect from pre-industrial times to 1950 and a small cooling effect afterward.

a. Global warming
b. Controlled Foreign Corporations
c. Consumer goods
d. Dividend unit

34. _____ exists when sales of identical goods or services are transacted at different prices from the same provider. In a theoretical market with perfect information, no transaction costs or prohibition on secondary exchange (or re-selling) to prevent arbitrage, _____ can only be a feature of monopoly and oligopoly markets, where market power can be exercised. Otherwise, the moment the seller tries to sell the same good at different prices, the buyer at the lower price can arbitrage by selling to the consumer buying at the higher price but with a tiny discount.

a. Loss leader
b. Transfer pricing
c. Lerner Index
d. Price discrimination

35. Economic _____ is defined as an excess distribution to any factor in a production process above that which is required to induce the factor into the process or any excess above that which is necessary to keep the factor in its current use..

Classical Factor _____ is primarily concerned with the fee paid for the use of fixed (e.g. natural) resources. The classical definition is expressed as any excess payment above that required to induce or provide for production.

a. 100-year flood
b. 130-30 fund
c. 1921 recession
d. Rent

36. In economics, _____ is the ability of a firm to alter the market price of a good or service. A firm with _____ can raise prices without losing all customers to competitors.

When a firm has _____ it faces a downward-sloping demand curve.

a. Pacman conjecture
b. Revenue-cap regulation
c. Price makers
d. Market power

Chapter 16. Interest Rates, Investments, and Capital Markets

37. In economics, _____ describes the state of a market with respect to competition.

- Perfect competition, in which the market consists of a very large number of firms producing a homogeneous product.
- Monopolistic competition where there are a large number of independent firms which have a very small proportion of the market share.
- Oligopoly, in which a market is dominated by a small number of firms which own more than 40% of the market share.
- Oligopsony, a market dominated by many sellers and a few buyers.
- Monopoly, where there is only one provider of a product or service.
- Natural monopoly, a monopoly in which economies of scale cause efficiency to increase continuously with the size of the firm. A firm is a natural monopoly if it is able to serve the entire market demand at a lower cost than any combination of two or more smaller, more specialized firms.
- Monopsony, when there is only one buyer in a market.

The imperfectly competitive structure is quite identical to the realistic market conditions where some monopolistic competitors, monopolists, oligopolists, and duopolists exist and dominate the market conditions. The elements of _____ include the number and size distribution of firms, entry conditions, and the extent of differentiation.

These somewhat abstract concerns tend to determine some but not all details of a specific concrete market system where buyers and sellers actually meet and commit to trade.

a. Market structure
b. Monopolistic competition
c. Labour economics
d. Human capital

38. _____ has several particular meanings:

- in mathematics
    - _____ function
    - Euler _____
    - _____
    - _____ subgroup
    - method of _____s (partial differential equations)
- in physics and engineering
    - any _____ curve that shows the relationship between certain input- and output parameters, e.g.
    - an I-V or current-voltage _____ is the current in a circuit as a function of the applied voltage
    - Receiver-Operator _____
- in fiction
    - in Dungeons ' Dragons, _____ is another name for ability score

a. Russian financial crisis
b. Demand
c. Technocracy
d. Characteristic

39. In economics, the _____ can be defined as the graph depicting the relationship between the price of a certain commodity, and the amount of it that consumers are willing and able to purchase at that given price. It is a graphic representation of a demand schedule. The _____ for all consumers together follows from the _____ of every individual consumer: the individual demands at each price are added together.

a. Wage curve
b. Cost curve
c. Kuznets curve
d. Demand curve

40. Competitive market equilibrium is the traditional concept of economic equilibrium, appropriate for the analysis of commodity markets with flexible prices and many traders, and serving as the benchmark of efficiency in economic analysis. It relies crucially on the assumption of a competitive environment where each trader decides upon a quantity that is so small compared to the total quantity traded in the market that their individual transactions have no influence on the prices.Competitive markets are an ideal, a standard that other market structures are evaluated by.

A _____ consists of a vector of prices and an allocation such that given the prices, each trader by maximizing his objective function (profit, preferences) subject to his technological possibilities and resource constraints plans to trade into his part of the proposed allocation, and such that the prices make all net trades compatible with one another ('clear the market') by equating aggregate supply and demand for the commodities which are traded.

a. Competitive equilibrium
b. Market system
c. Product-Market Growth Matrix
d. Partial equilibrium

41. _____ theory is a branch of theoretical economics. It seeks to explain the behavior of supply, demand and prices in a whole economy with several or many markets. It is often assumed that agents are price takers and in that setting two common notions of equilibrium exist: Walrasian (or competitive) equilibrium, and its generalization; a price equilibrium with transfers.
a. Rational choice theory
b. New Keynesian economics
c. Human capital
d. General equilibrium

42. An _____ is a retirement plan account that provides some tax advantages for retirement savings in the United States.

Chapter 16. Interest Rates, Investments, and Capital Markets

There are a number of different types of _____s, which may be either employer-provided or self-provided plans. The types include:

- Roth _____ - contributions are made with after-tax assets, all transactions within the _____ have no tax impact, and withdrawals are usually tax-free. Named for Senator William Roth.
- Traditional _____ - contributions are often tax-deductible (often simplified as 'money is deposited before tax' or 'contributions are made with pre-tax assets'), all transactions and earnings within the _____ have no tax impact, and withdrawals at retirement are taxed as income (except for those portions of the withdrawal corresponding to contributions that were not deducted.) Depending upon the nature of the contribution, a traditional _____ may be referred to as a 'deductible _____' or a 'non-deductible _____.'
- SEP _____ - a provision that allows an employer (typically a small business or self-employed individual) to make retirement plan contributions into a Traditional _____ established in the employee's name, instead of to a pension fund account in the company's name.
- SIMPLE _____ - a simplified employee pension plan that allows both employer and employee contributions, similar to a 401(k) plan, but with lower contribution limits and simpler (and thus less costly) administration. Although it is termed an _____, it is treated separately.
- Self-Directed _____ - a self-directed _____ that permits the account holder to make investments on behalf of the retirement plan.

There are two other subtypes of _____, named Rollover _____ and Conduit _____, that are viewed as obsolete under current tax law (their functions have been subsumed by the Traditional _____) by some; but this tax law is set to expire unless extended. However, some individuals still maintain these accounts in order to keep track of the source of these assets.

a. Individual Retirement Arrangement
c. AD-IA Model

b. ACEA agreement
d. ACCRA Cost of Living Index

43. In economics, economic equilibrium is simply a state of the world where economic forces are balanced and in the absence of external influences the (equilibrium) values of economic variables will not change. It is the point at which quantity demanded and quantity supplied are equal. _____, for example, refers to a condition where a market price is established through competition such that the amount of goods or services sought by buyers is equal to the amount of goods or services produced by sellers.

a. Marketization
c. Product-Market Growth Matrix

b. Market equilibrium
d. Regulated market

44. In economics, game theory, and decision theory the _____ theorem or _____ hypothesis predicts that the 'betting preferences' of people with regard to uncertain outcomes (gambles) can be described by a mathematical relation which takes into account the size of a payout (whether in money or other goods), the probability of occurrence, risk aversion, and the different utility of the same payout to people with different assets or personal preferences. It is a more sophisticated theory than simply predicting that choices will be made based on expected value (which takes into account only the size of the payout and the probability of occurrence.)

Daniel Bernoulli described the complete theory in 1738.

a. Ordinal utility
c. Utility
b. Expected utility hypothesis
d. Expected utility

45. In economics, _____ is a measure of the relative satisfaction from consumption of various goods and services. Given this measure, one may speak meaningfully of increasing or decreasing _____, and thereby explain economic behavior in terms of attempts to increase one's _____. For illustrative purposes, changes in _____ are sometimes expressed in units called utils.

a. Utility function
c. Ordinal utility
b. Expected utility hypothesis
d. Utility

Chapter 17. Uncertainty

1. In economics, game theory, and decision theory the _____ theorem or _____ hypothesis predicts that the 'betting preferences' of people with regard to uncertain outcomes (gambles) can be described by a mathematical relation which takes into account the size of a payout (whether in money or other goods), the probability of occurrence, risk aversion, and the different utility of the same payout to people with different assets or personal preferences. It is a more sophisticated theory than simply predicting that choices will be made based on expected value (which takes into account only the size of the payout and the probability of occurrence.)

Daniel Bernoulli described the complete theory in 1738.

    a. Utility   b. Ordinal utility
    c. Expected utility   d. Expected utility hypothesis

2. In economics, _____ is the active redirecting resources from being consumed today so that they may create benefits in the future; the use of assets to earn income or profit. _____ is the process of making an investment in order to earn a profit, for example equity investment either through a fund, a 401k plan, or individually. People often invest in order to build up their estate or to accumulate funds for retirement.

To try to predict good stocks to invest in, two main schools of thought exist: technical analysis and fundamentals analysis.

    a. ACEA agreement   b. AD-IA Model
    c. Investing   d. ACCRA Cost of Living Index

3. In economics, _____ is a measure of the relative satisfaction from consumption of various goods and services. Given this measure, one may speak meaningfully of increasing or decreasing _____, and thereby explain economic behavior in terms of attempts to increase one's _____. For illustrative purposes, changes in _____ are sometimes expressed in units called utils.

    a. Ordinal utility   b. Expected utility hypothesis
    c. Utility function   d. Utility

4. _____ is a way of expressing knowledge or belief that an event will occur or has occurred. In mathematics the concept has been given an exact meaning in _____ theory, that is used extensively in such areas of study as mathematics, statistics, finance, gambling, science, and philosophy to draw conclusions about the likelihood of potential events and the underlying mechanics of complex systems.

The word _____ does not have a consistent direct definition.

    a. 1921 recession   b. 130-30 fund
    c. Probability   d. 100-year flood

5. In probability theory and statistics, a _____ identifies either the probability of each value of an unidentified random variable (when the variable is discrete), or the probability of the value falling within a particular interval (when the variable is continuous.) The _____ describes the range of possible values that a random variable can attain and the probability that the value of the random variable is within any (measurable) subset of that range. The Normal distribution, often called the 'bell curve'

Chapter 17. Uncertainty

When the random variable takes values in the set of real numbers, the _____ is completely described by the cumulative distribution function, whose value at each real x is the probability that the random variable is smaller than or equal to x.

a. Probability distribution
b. 130-30 fund
c. 100-year flood
d. 1921 recession

6. In probability theory and statistics, the _____ (or expectation value or mean and for continuous random variables with a density function it is the probability density -weighted integral of the possible values.

The term '_____' can be misleading.

a. AD-IA Model
b. ACCRA Cost of Living Index
c. ACEA agreement
d. Expected value

7. _____ is the a method of technical and economic research of the systems for purpose to optimize a parity between system's consumer functions or properties and expenses to achieve those functions or properties.

This methodology for continuous perfection of production, industrial technologies, organizational structures was developed by Juryj Sobolev in 1948 at the 'Perm telephone factory'

- 1948 Juryj Sobolev - the first success in application of a method analysis at the 'Perm telephone factory'.
- 1949 - the first application for the invention as result of use of the new method.

Today in economically developed countries practically each enterprise or the company use methodology of the kind of functional-cost analysis as a practice of the quality management, most full satisfying to principles of standards of series ISO 9000.

- Interest of consumer not in products itself, but the advantage which it will receive from its usage.
- The consumer aspires to reduce his expenses
- Functions needed by consumer can be executed in the various ways, and, hence, with various efficiency and expenses. Among possible alternatives of realization of functions exist such in which the parity of quality and the price is the optimal for the consumer.

The goal of _____ is achievement of the highest consumer satisfaction of production at simultaneous decrease in all kinds of industrial expenses Classical _____ has three English synonyms - Value Engineering, Value Management, Value Analysis.

a. Staple financing
b. Monopoly wage
c. Willingness to pay
d. Function cost analysis

8. In probability theory and statistics, _____ is a measure of the variability or dispersion of a population, a data set, or a probability distribution. A low _____ indicates that the data points tend to be very close to the same value (the mean), while high _____ indicates that the data are 'spread out' over a large range of values.

For example, the average height for adult men in the United States is about 70 inches, with a _____ of around 3 inches.

a. Standard deviation
b. 1921 recession
c. 130-30 fund
d. 100-year flood

9. In statistics, _____ has two related meanings:

- the arithmetic _____
- the expected value of a random variable, which is also called the population _____.

It is sometimes stated that the '_____' _____s average. This is incorrect if '_____' is taken in the specific sense of 'arithmetic _____' as there are different types of averages: the _____, median, and mode. Other simple statistical analyses use measures of spread, such as range, interquartile range, or standard deviation. For a real-valued random variable X, the _____ is the expectation of X. Note that not every probability distribution has a defined _____ (or variance); see the Cauchy distribution for an example.

a. Mean
b. 130-30 fund
c. 1921 recession
d. 100-year flood

10. _____ is a concept in economics, finance, and psychology related to the behaviour of consumers and investors under uncertainty. _____ is the reluctance of a person to accept a bargain with an uncertain payoff rather than another bargain with a more certain, but possibly lower, expected payoff. For example, a risk-averse investor might choose to put his or her money into a bank account with a low but guaranteed interest rate, rather than into a stock that is likely to have high returns, but also has a chance of becoming worthless.

a. Risk aversion
b. Risk theory
c. Reinsurance
d. Compound annual growth rate

11. A _____ is the minimum difference a person requires to be willing to take an uncertain bet, between the expected value of the bet and the certain value that he is indifferent to.

The certainty equivalent is the guaranteed payoff at which a person is 'indifferent' between accepting the guaranteed payoff and a higher but uncertain payoff. (It is the amount of the higher payout minus the _____.)

a. Risk premium
b. Ruin theory
c. Linear model
d. Workers compensation

12. While preferences are the conventional foundation of microeconomics, it is often convenient to represent preferences with a _____ and reason indirectly about preferences with _____s. Let X be the consumption set, the set of all mutually-exclusive packages the consumer could conceivably consume (such as an indifference curve map without the indifference curves.) The consumer's _____ $u : X \to \mathbf{R}$ ranks each package in the consumption set.

a. Expected utility hypothesis
b. Utility
c. Ordinal utility
d. Utility function

Chapter 17. Uncertainty

13. In statistics, _____ indicates the strength and direction of a linear relationship between two random variables. That is in contrast with the usage of the term in colloquial speech, which denotes any relationship, not necessarily linear. In general statistical usage, _____ or co-relation refers to the departure of two random variables from independence.
   a. Correlation
   b. 100-year flood
   c. 1921 recession
   d. 130-30 fund

14. _____ is an equity (stock) exchange located at 11 Wall Street in lower Manhattan, New York, USA. It is the largest stock exchange in the world by dollar value of its listed companies' securities. As of October 2008, the combined capitalization of all domestic _____ listed companies was US$10.1 trillion.
   a. 100-year flood
   b. 130-30 fund
   c. 1921 recession
   d. New York Stock Exchange

15. A _____ is a corporation or mutual organization which provides trading facilities for stock brokers and traders, to trade stocks and other securities. It may be a physical trading room where the traders gather, or a formalised communications network. Creation of a _____ is a strategy of economic development.
   a. 100-year flood
   b. Primary shares
   c. Stock Exchange
   d. SEAQ

16. A _____ or equity fund is a fund that invests in equities more commonly known as stocks. _____s are contrasted with bond funds and money funds. Fund assets are typically mainly in stock, with some amount of cash, which is generally quite small, as opposed to bonds, notes, or other securities.
   a. Vulture fund
   b. Stock fund
   c. Lipper average
   d. Mutual fund fees and expenses

17. _____, in law and economics, is a form of risk management primarily used to hedge against the risk of a contingent loss. _____ is defined as the equitable transfer of the risk of a loss, from one entity to another, in exchange for a premium, and can be thought of as a guaranteed small loss to prevent a large, possibly devastating loss. An insurer is a company selling the _____; an insured or policyholder is the person or entity buying the _____.
   a. AD-IA Model
   b. ACCRA Cost of Living Index
   c. Insurance
   d. ACEA agreement

18. _____, anti-selection insurance, statistics, and risk management. It refers to a market process in which 'bad' results occur when buyers and sellers have asymmetric information (i.e. access to different information): the 'bad' products or customers are more likely to be selected. A bank that sets one price for all its checking account customers runs the risk of being adversely selected against by its low-balance, high-activity (and hence least profitable) customers.
   a. ACCRA Cost of Living Index
   b. AD-IA Model
   c. Adverse selection
   d. ACEA agreement

19. _____ is a financial mechanism in which a debtor obtains the right to delay payments to a creditor, for a defined period of time, in exchange for a charge or fee. Essentially, the party that owes money in the present purchases the right to delay the payment until some future date. The discount, or charge, is simply the difference between the original amount owed in the present and the amount that has to be paid in the future to settle the debt.
   a. Certified Risk Manager
   b. Maximum life span
   c. Generalized linear model
   d. Discounting

20. _____ or net present worth (NPW) is defined as the total present value (PV) of a time series of cash flows. It is a standard method for using the time value of money to appraise long-term projects. Used for capital budgeting, and widely throughout economics, it measures the excess or shortfall of cash flows, in present value terms, once financing charges are met.

   a. Future value
   b. Maturity
   c. Refinancing risk
   d. Net present value

21. _____ is the value on a given date of a future payment or series of future payments, discounted to reflect the time value of money and other factors such as investment risk. _____ calculations are widely used in business and economics to provide a means to compare cash flows at different times on a meaningful 'like to like' basis.

Money value fluctuates over time: $100 today are not worth $100 in five years.

   a. Future value
   b. Present value of costs
   c. Tax shield
   d. Present value

Chapter 18. Externalities, Open-Access, and Public Goods

1. In economics, an _____ is any good or commodity, transported from one country to another country in a legitimate fashion, typically for use in trade. _____ goods or services are provided to foreign consumers by domestic producers. _____ is an important part of international trade.
   a. AD-IA Model
   b. ACEA agreement
   c. ACCRA Cost of Living Index
   d. Export

2. An _____ is a tax levied on the financial income of people, corporations, or other legal entities. Various _____ systems exist, with varying degrees of tax incidence. Income taxation can be progressive, proportional, or regressive.
   a. Income tax
   b. AD-IA Model
   c. ACCRA Cost of Living Index
   d. ACEA agreement

3. A _____ is the exclusive authority to determine how a resource is used, whether that resource is owned by government or by individuals. All economic goods have a _____s attribute. This attribute has three broad components

   1. The right to use the good
   2. The right to earn income from the good
   3. The right to transfer the good to others

   The concept of _____s as used by economists and legal scholars are related but distinct. The distinction is largely seen in the economists' focus on the ability of an individual or collective to control the use of the good.

   a. Post-sale restraint
   b. High-reeve
   c. Holder in due course
   d. Property right

4. In economics, a _____ is a good that is non-rivaled and non-excludable. This means, respectively, that consumption of the good by one individual does not reduce availability of the good for consumption by others; and that no one can be effectively excluded from using the good. In the real world, there may be no such thing as an absolutely non-rivaled and non-excludable good; but economists think that some goods approximate the concept closely enough for the analysis to be economically useful.
   a. Public good
   b. Happiness economics
   c. Neoclassical synthesis
   d. Demand-pull theory

5. A _____ is a consumption tax charged at the point of purchase for certain goods and services. The tax is usually set as a percentage by the government charging the tax. There is usually a list of exemptions.
   a. 130-30 fund
   b. 1921 recession
   c. 100-year flood
   d. Sales tax

6. To _____ is to impose a financial charge or other levy upon a taxpayer by a state or the functional equivalent of a state.

   _____es are also imposed by many subnational entities. _____es consist of direct _____ or indirect _____, and may be paid in money or as its labour equivalent (often but not always unpaid.)

   a. 100-year flood
   b. 1921 recession
   c. 130-30 fund
   d. Tax

7. To tax is to impose a financial charge or other levy upon a taxpayer by a state or the functional equivalent of a state.

_____ are also imposed by many subnational entities. _____ consist of direct tax or indirect tax, and may be paid in money or as its labour equivalent (often but not always unpaid.)

a. 100-year flood
b. Taxes
c. 1921 recession
d. 130-30 fund

8. In economics, a common-pool resource, alternatively termed a _____ resource, is a particular type of good consisting of a natural or human-made resource system, the size or characteristics of which makes it costly, but not impossible, to exclude potential beneficiaries from obtaining benefits from its use. Unlike pure public goods, common pool resources face problems of congestion or overuse, because they are subtractable. A common-pool resource typically consists of a core resource, which defines the stock variable, while providing a limited quantity of extractable fringe units, which defines the flow variable.

a. Government monopoly
b. Common-pool resource
c. Price-cap regulation
d. Common property

9. Economics:

- _____, the desire to own something and the ability to pay for it
- _____ curve, a graphic representation of a _____ schedule
- _____ deposit, the money in checking accounts
- _____ pull theory, the theory that inflation occurs when _____ for goods and services exceeds existing supplies
- _____ schedule, a table that lists the quantity of a good a person will buy it each different price
- _____ side economics, the school of economics at believes government spending and tax cuts open economy by raising _____

a. McKesson ' Robbins scandal
b. Variability
c. Production
d. Demand

10. A _____ is an object whose consumption increases the utility of the consumer, for which the quantity demanded exceeds the quantity supplied at zero price. _____s are usually modeled as having diminishing marginal utility. The first individual purchase has high utility; the second has less.

a. Good
b. Pie method
c. Composite good
d. Merit good

Chapter 18. Externalities, Open-Access, and Public Goods

11. In economics, _____ describes the state of a market with respect to competition.

   - Perfect competition, in which the market consists of a very large number of firms producing a homogeneous product.
   - Monopolistic competition where there are a large number of independent firms which have a very small proportion of the market share.
   - Oligopoly, in which a market is dominated by a small number of firms which own more than 40% of the market share.
   - Oligopsony, a market dominated by many sellers and a few buyers.
   - Monopoly, where there is only one provider of a product or service.
   - Natural monopoly, a monopoly in which economies of scale cause efficiency to increase continuously with the size of the firm. A firm is a natural monopoly if it is able to serve the entire market demand at a lower cost than any combination of two or more smaller, more specialized firms.
   - Monopsony, when there is only one buyer in a market.

The imperfectly competitive structure is quite identical to the realistic market conditions where some monopolistic competitors, monopolists, oligopolists, and duopolists exist and dominate the market conditions. The elements of _____ include the number and size distribution of firms, entry conditions, and the extent of differentiation.

These somewhat abstract concerns tend to determine some but not all details of a specific concrete market system where buyers and sellers actually meet and commit to trade.

   a. Market structure
   c. Labour economics
   b. Monopolistic competition
   d. Human capital

12. Many _____ are related to the environmental consequences of production and use

   - Systemic risk describes the risks to the overall economy arising from the risks which the banking system takes. That the private costs of banking failure may be smaller than the social costs justifies banking regulations, although regulations could create a moral hazard.

   - Anthropogenic climate change is attributed to greenhouse gas emissions from burning oil, gas, and coal. Global warming has been ranked as the #1 externality of all economic activity, in the magnitude of potential harms and yet remains unmitigated.

   a. White certificates
   c. Total Economic Value
   b. Green certificate
   d. Negative externalities

144 Chapter 18. Externalities, Open-Access, and Public Goods

13. Examples of _____ include:

    - A beekeeper keeps the bees for their honey. A side effect or externality associated with his activity is the pollination of surrounding crops by the bees. The value generated by the pollination may be more important than the value of the harvested honey.

    - An individual planting an attractive garden in front of his house may provide benefits to others living in the area, and even financial benefits in the form of increased property values for all property owners.

    - An individual buying a product that is interconnected in a network (e.g., a video cellphone) will increase the usefulness of such phones to other people who have a video cellphone. When each new user of a product increases the value of the same product owned by others, the phenomenon is called a network externality or a network effect. Network externalities often have 'tipping points' where, suddenly, the product reaches general acceptance and near-universal usage, a phenomenon which can be seen in the near universal take-up of cellphones in some Scandinavian countries.

    - Knowledge spillover of inventions and information - once an invention (or most other forms of practical information) is discovered or made more easily accessible, others benefit by exploiting the invention or information. Copyright and intellectual property law are mechanisms to allow the inventor or creator to benefit from a temporary, state-protected monopoly in return for 'sharing' the information through publication or other means.

    a. Positive externalities
    c. Weighted average cost of carbon
    b. Total Economic Value
    d. Negative externalities

14. _____ has several particular meanings:

    - in mathematics
        - _____ function
        - Euler _____
        - _____
        - _____ subgroup
        - method of _____ s (partial differential equations)
    - in physics and engineering
        - any _____ curve that shows the relationship between certain input- and output parameters, e.g.
        - an I-V or current-voltage _____ is the current in a circuit as a function of the applied voltage
        - Receiver-Operator _____
    - in fiction
        - in Dungeons ' Dragons, _____ is another name for ability score

    a. Technocracy
    c. Characteristic
    b. Russian financial crisis
    d. Demand

Chapter 18. Externalities, Open-Access, and Public Goods   145

15. In economics, _____ is a measure of the relative satisfaction from consumption of various goods and services. Given this measure, one may speak meaningfully of increasing or decreasing _____, and thereby explain economic behavior in terms of attempts to increase one's _____. For illustrative purposes, changes in _____ are sometimes expressed in units called utils.

   a. Utility
   b. Ordinal utility
   c. Utility function
   d. Expected utility hypothesis

16. In economics and finance, _____ is the change in total cost that arises when the quantity produced changes by one unit. It is the cost of producing one more unit of a good. Mathematically, the _____ function is expressed as the first derivative of the total cost (TC) function with respect to quantity (Q.)

   a. Khozraschyot
   b. Marginal cost
   c. Variable cost
   d. Quality costs

17. In economics, a _____ exists when the production or use of goods and services by the market is not efficient. That is, there exists another outcome where all involved can be made better off. _____s can be viewed as scenarios where individuals' pursuit of pure self-interest leads to results that are not efficient - that can be improved upon from the societal point-of-view.

   a. General equilibrium
   b. Market failure
   c. Fixed exchange rate
   d. Financial economics

18. In economics _____ is defined as the sum of private and external costs. Economic theorists ascribe individual decision-making to a calculation costs and benefits. Rational choice theory assumes that individuals only consider their own private costs when making decisions, not the costs that may be borne by others.

   a. Khozraschyot
   b. Psychic cost
   c. Cost-Volume-Profit Analysis
   d. Social cost

19. Necessary _____s:

If x is a necessary _____ of y, then the presence of y necessarily implies the presence of x. The presence of x, however, does not imply that y will occur.

Sufficient _____s:

If x is a sufficient _____ of y, then the presence of x necessarily implies the presence of y.

   a. Political philosophy
   b. Philosophy of economics
   c. Materialism
   d. Cause

20. Competitive market equilibrium is the traditional concept of economic equilibrium, appropriate for the analysis of commodity markets with flexible prices and many traders, and serving as the benchmark of efficiency in economic analysis. It relies crucially on the assumption of a competitive environment where each trader decides upon a quantity that is so small compared to the total quantity traded in the market that their individual transactions have no influence on the prices.Competitive markets are an ideal, a standard that other market structures are evaluated by.

A _____ consists of a vector of prices and an allocation such that given the prices, each trader by maximizing his objective function (profit, preferences) subject to his technological possibilities and resource constraints plans to trade into his part of the proposed allocation, and such that the prices make all net trades compatible with one another ('clear the market') by equating aggregate supply and demand for the commodities which are traded.

   a. Market system
   b. Competitive equilibrium
   c. Product-Market Growth Matrix
   d. Partial equilibrium

21. _____ theory is a branch of theoretical economics. It seeks to explain the behavior of supply, demand and prices in a whole economy with several or many markets. It is often assumed that agents are price takers and in that setting two common notions of equilibrium exist: Walrasian (or competitive) equilibrium, and its generalization; a price equilibrium with transfers.

   a. Rational choice theory
   b. New Keynesian economics
   c. Human capital
   d. General equilibrium

22. In economics, economic equilibrium is simply a state of the world where economic forces are balanced and in the absence of external influences the (equilibrium) values of economic variables will not change. It is the point at which quantity demanded and quantity supplied are equal. _____, for example, refers to a condition where a market price is established through competition such that the amount of goods or services sought by buyers is equal to the amount of goods or services produced by sellers.

   a. Product-Market Growth Matrix
   b. Market equilibrium
   c. Regulated market
   d. Marketization

23. The term surplus is used in economics for several related quantities. The consumer surplus is the amount that consumers benefit by being able to purchase a product for a price that is less than they would be willing to pay. The _____ is the amount that producers benefit by selling at a market price mechanism that is higher than they would be willing to sell for.

   a. Long term
   b. Schedule delay
   c. Returns to scale
   d. Producer surplus

24. A _____ describes one of a number of pieces of legislation relating to the reduction of smog and air pollution in general. The use by governments to enforce clean air standards has contributed to an improvement in human health and longer life spans. Critics argue it has also sapped corporate profits and contributed to outsourcing, while defenders counter that improved environmental air quality has generated more jobs than it has eliminated.

   a. Smog
   b. Clean Air Act
   c. 100-year flood
   d. 130-30 fund

25. The _____ is a United States federal law that requires the Environmental Protection Agency (EPA) to develop and enforce regulations to protect the general public from exposure to airborne contaminants that are known to be hazardous to human health. This law is an amendment to the Clean Air Act (CAA) originally passed in 1963.

   a. Beneficial ownership
   b. Competition law
   c. Meat Inspection Act
   d. Clean Air Act Extension of 1970

Chapter 18. Externalities, Open-Access, and Public Goods

26. _____ is a practice of protecting the environment, on individual, organisational or governmental level, for the benefit of the natural environment and (or) humans.

Due to the pressures of population and technology the biophysical environment is being degraded, sometimes permanently. This has been recognised and governments began placing restraints on activities that caused environmental degradation.

   a. ACEA agreement
   b. ACCRA Cost of Living Index
   c. AD-IA Model
   d. Environmental protection

27. In economics, _____ is equal to total cost divided by the number of goods produced (the output quantity, Q.) It is also equal to the sum of average variable costs (total variable costs divided by Q) plus average fixed costs (total fixed costs divided by Q.) _____s may be dependent on the time period considered (increasing production may be expensive or impossible in the short term, for example.)
   a. Average fixed cost
   b. Average cost
   c. Average variable cost
   d. Explicit cost

28. In economics, a _____ is a graph of the costs of production as a function of total quantity produced. In a free market economy, productively efficient firms use these curves to find the optimal point of production, where they make the most profits. There are a few different types of _____s, each relevant to a different area of economics.
   a. Demand curve
   b. Cost curve
   c. Kuznets curve
   d. Phillips curve

29. Under the system of feudalism, a _____, fief, feud, feoff often consisted of inheritable lands or revenue-producing property granted by a liege lord, generally to a vassal, in return for a form of allegiance, originally to give him the means to fulfill his military duties when called upon. However anything of value could be held in fief, such as an office, a right of exploitation (e.g., hunting, fishing) or any other type of revenue, rather than the land it comes from.

Originally, the feudal institution of vassalage did not imply the giving or receiving of landholdings (which were granted only as a reward for loyalty), but by the eighth century the giving of a landholding was becoming standard.

   a. 130-30 fund
   b. Fiefdom
   c. 1921 recession
   d. 100-year flood

30. In economics, an _____ or spillover of an economic transaction is an impact on a party that is not directly involved in the transaction. In such a case, prices do not reflect the full costs or benefits in production or consumption of a product or service. A positive impact is called an external benefit, while a negative impact is called an external cost.
   a. Environmental tariff
   b. Environmental impact assessment
   c. Existence value
   d. Externality

31. An _____ is a tax based on the value of real estate or personal property. It is more common than the opposite, a specific duty, or a tax based on the quantity of an item regardless of price.

Chapter 18. Externalities, Open-Access, and Public Goods

An _____ is typically imposed at the time of a transaction), but it may be imposed on an annual basis (real or personal property tax) or in connection with another significant event (inheritance tax, surrendering citizenship, or tariffs.)

    a. User charge   b. Indirect tax
    c. Ad valorem tax   d. Optimal tax

32. A _____ is a duty imposed on goods when they are moved across a political boundary. They are usually associated with protectionism, the economic policy of restraining trade between nations. For political reasons, _____s are usually imposed on imported goods, although they may also be imposed on exported goods.

    a. 100-year flood   b. 130-30 fund
    c. 1921 recession   d. Tariff

33. _____, short for Ecological taxation, can refer to:

A policy that introduces taxes intended to promote ecologically sustainable activities via economic incentives. Such a policy can complement or avert the need for regulatory approaches. Often, such a policy intends to maintain overall tax revenue by proportionately reducing other taxes, e.g. on human labor and renewable resources, in which case it is known as the green tax shift towards ecological taxation.

    a. AD-IA Model   b. ACEA agreement
    c. Ecotax   d. ACCRA Cost of Living Index

34. A _____ refers to property being sold by a taxing authority or the court to recover delinquent taxes.

When property taxes are not paid, title gets transferred to the state. The owner will then have a period of time to redeem the property by paying the overdue taxes, including penalties and costs.

    a. Tax wedge   b. Tax competition
    c. Tax Sale   d. Taxation as theft

35. _____ is a common concept in economics, and gives rise to derived concepts such as consumer debt. Generally _____ is defined by opposition to production. But the precise definition can vary because different schools of economists define production quite differently.

    a. Federal Reserve Bank Notes   b. Foreclosure data providers
    c. Cash or share options   d. Consumption

36. _____ is a term that refers both to:

- a formal discipline used to help appraise, or assess, the case for a project or proposal, which itself is a process known as project appraisal; and
- an informal approach to making decisions of any kind.

Chapter 18. Externalities, Open-Access, and Public Goods

Under both definitions the process involves, whether explicitly or implicitly, weighing the total expected costs against the total expected benefits of one or more actions in order to choose the best or most profitable option. The formal process is often referred to as either CBA (_____) or BCost-benefit analysis

A hallmark of CBA is that all benefits and all costs are expressed in money terms, and are adjusted for the time value of money, so that all flows of benefits and flows of project costs over time (which tend to occur at different points in time) are expressed on a common basis in terms of their e;present value.e; Closely related, but slightly different, formal techniques include Cost-effectiveness analysis, Economic impact analysis, Fiscal impact analysis and Social Return on Investment(SROI) analysis. The latter builds upon the logic of _____, but differs in that it is explicitly designed to inform the practical decision-making of enterprise managers and investors focused on optimising their social and environmental impacts.

    a. Decision theory
    b. 130-30 fund
    c. 100-year flood
    d. Cost-benefit analysis

37. _____ is a common market structure where many competing producers sell products that are differentiated from one another (ie. the products are substitutes, but are not exactly alike.) Many markets are monopolistically competitive, common examples include the markets for restaurants, cereal, clothing, shoes and service industries in large cities.

    a. Perfect competition
    b. Financial crisis
    c. Mathematical economics
    d. Monopolistic competition

38. In law and economics, the _____, describes the economic efficiency of an economic allocation or outcome in the presence of externalities. The theorem states that when trade in an externality is possible and there are no transaction costs, bargaining will lead to an efficient outcome regardless of the initial allocation of property rights. In practice, obstacles to bargaining or poorly defined property rights can prevent Coasian bargaining.

    a. Coase Theorem
    b. Means test
    c. Prior appropriation water rights
    d. General Mining Act of 1872

39. _____ is an administrative approach used to control pollution by providing economic incentives for achieving reductions in the emissions of pollutants. It is sometimes called cap and trade. A coal power plant in Germany.

    a. International Climate Science Coalition
    b. Efficient energy use
    c. Emissions trading
    d. ACCRA Cost of Living Index

40. The Court of Justice of the European Communities, usually called the _____, is the highest court in the European Union in matters of European Community law. It has the ultimate say on matters of EU law in order to ensure its equal application across all EU member states.

The court was established in 1952 and is -- unlike most other Union institutions -- based in Luxembourg.

    a. European Court of Justice
    b. ACCRA Cost of Living Index
    c. European Union
    d. ACEA agreement

41. The _____ is an economic and political union of 27 member states, located primarily in Europe. It was established by the Treaty of Maastricht on 1 November 1993, upon the foundations of the pre-existing European Economic Community. With a population of almost 500 million, the _____ generates an estimated 30% share (US$18.4 trillion in 2008) of the nominal gross world product.
   a. ACCRA Cost of Living Index
   b. ACEA agreement
   c. European Court of Justice
   d. European Union

42. _____ are gases in an atmosphere that absorb and emit radiation within the thermal infrared range. This process is the fundamental cause of the greenhouse effect. Common _____ in the Earth's atmosphere include water vapor, carbon dioxide, methane, nitrous oxide, ozone, and chlorofluorocarbons.
   a. G8 Climate Change Roundtable
   b. Post-Kyoto negotiations
   c. Greenhouse gases
   d. Carbon emissions trading

43. _____ is the point where a person stops employment completely. A person may also semi-retire and keep some sort of _____ job, out of choice rather than necessity. This usually happens upon reaching a determined age, when physical conditions don't allow the person to work any more (by illness or accident), or even for personal choice (usually in the presence of an adequate pension or personal savings.)
   a. Termination of employment
   b. 100-year flood
   c. Layoff
   d. Retirement

44. A _____ is defined in economics as a good that exhibits these properties:

   - Excludable - it is reasonably possible to prevent a class of consumers (e.g. those who have not paid for it) from consuming the good.
   - Rivalrous - consumptions by one consumer prevents simultaneous consumption by other consumers. _____s satisfies an individual want while public good satisfies a collective want of the society.

   A _____ is the opposite of a public good, as they are almost exclusively made for profit.

   An example of the _____ is bread: bread eaten by a given person cannot be consumed by another (rivalry), and it is easy for a baker to refuse to trade a loaf (excludable

   a. Pie method
   b. Private good
   c. Demerit good
   d. Positional goods

45. _____ are a type of good in economics, sometimes classified as a subtype of public goods that are excludable but non-rivalrous, at least until reaching a point where congestion occurs. These goods are often provided by a natural monopoly.

   Examples of _____ would include private golf courses, cinemas, cable television, access to copyrighted works, and the services provided by social or religious clubs to their members.

   a. NOPAT
   b. January effect
   c. Correlation trading
   d. Club goods

46. In economics, the _____ can be defined as the graph depicting the relationship between the price of a certain commodity, and the amount of it that consumers are willing and able to purchase at that given price. It is a graphic representation of a demand schedule. The _____ for all consumers together follows from the _____ of every individual consumer: the individual demands at each price are added together.
   a. Kuznets curve
   c. Wage curve
   b. Cost curve
   d. Demand curve

47. _____ is a term used in the stock-trading world to describe the practice of buying shares or other securities without actually having the capital to cover the trade. This is possible when recently bought or sold shares are unsettled, and therefore have not been paid for.

Since stock transactions usually settle after three business days, a crafty trader can buy a stock and sell it the following day, without ever having sufficient funds in the account.

   a. Santa Claus rally
   c. Barbell strategy
   b. Multilateral Trading Facility
   d. Free riding

Chapter 19. Asymmetric Information

1. _____, anti-selection insurance, statistics, and risk management. It refers to a market process in which 'bad' results occur when buyers and sellers have asymmetric information (i.e. access to different information): the 'bad' products or customers are more likely to be selected. A bank that sets one price for all its checking account customers runs the risk of being adversely selected against by its low-balance, high-activity (and hence least profitable) customers.
   a. ACEA agreement
   b. ACCRA Cost of Living Index
   c. AD-IA Model
   d. Adverse selection

2. A _____ is an object whose consumption increases the utility of the consumer, for which the quantity demanded exceeds the quantity supplied at zero price. _____s are usually modeled as having diminishing marginal utility. The first individual purchase has high utility; the second has less.
   a. Merit good
   b. Composite good
   c. Pie method
   d. Good

3. The _____ describes a firm's market power. It is defined by:

$$L = \frac{P - MC}{P}$$

where P is the market price set by the firm and MC is the firm's marginal cost. The index ranges from a high of 1 to a low of 0, with higher numbers implying greater market power.

   a. Lerner Index
   b. Two-part tariff
   c. Discounts and allowances
   d. Break even analysis

4. _____ is the prospect that a party insulated from risk may behave differently from the way it would behave if it were fully exposed to the risk. In insurance, _____ that occurs without conscious or malicious action is called morale hazard.

_____ is related to information asymmetry, a situation in which one party in a transaction has more information than another.

   a. Moral hazard
   b. 100-year flood
   c. 130-30 fund
   d. 1921 recession

5. _____ in economics and business is the result of an exchange and from that trade we assign a numerical monetary value to a good, service or asset. If Alice trades Bob 4 apples for an orange, the _____ of an orange is 4 apples. Inversely, the _____ of an apple is 1/4 oranges.
   a. Price
   b. Price book
   c. Premium pricing
   d. Price war

6. _____ exists when sales of identical goods or services are transacted at different prices from the same provider. In a theoretical market with perfect information, no transaction costs or prohibition on secondary exchange (or re-selling) to prevent arbitrage, _____ can only be a feature of monopoly and oligopoly markets, where market power can be exercised. Otherwise, the moment the seller tries to sell the same good at different prices, the buyer at the lower price can arbitrage by selling to the consumer buying at the higher price but with a tiny discount.
   a. Transfer pricing
   b. Price discrimination
   c. Lerner Index
   d. Loss leader

Chapter 19. Asymmetric Information

7. In game theory, _____ is communication between players which does not directly affect the payoffs of the game. This is in contrast to signaling in which sending certain messages may be costly for the sender depending on the state of the world. The classic example is of an expert (say, ecological) trying to explain the state of the world to an uninformed decision maker (say, politician voting on a deforestation bill.)
   a. Manipulated Nash equilibrium
   b. Cheap talk
   c. Screening game
   d. Complete mixing

8. _____ is a broad label that refers to any individuals or households that use goods and services generated within the economy. The concept of a _____ is used in different contexts, so that the usage and significance of the term may vary.

Typically when business people and economists talk of _____s they are talking about person as _____, an aggregated commodity item with little individuality other than that expressed in the buy/not-buy decision.

   a. 100-year flood
   b. 1921 recession
   c. Consumer
   d. 130-30 fund

9. In economics, _____ is the ability of a firm to alter the market price of a good or service. A firm with _____ can raise prices without losing all customers to competitors.

When a firm has _____ it faces a downward-sloping demand curve.

   a. Pacman conjecture
   b. Market power
   c. Price makers
   d. Revenue-cap regulation

10. The _____ is an independent agency of the United States government, established in 1914 by the _____ Act. Its principal mission is the promotion of 'consumer protection' and the elimination and prevention of what regulators perceive to be harmfully 'anti-competitive' business practices, such as coercive monopoly.

The _____ Act was one of President Wilson's major acts against trusts.

   a. 130-30 fund
   b. 1921 recession
   c. 100-year flood
   d. Federal Trade Commission

11. _____, in law and economics, is a form of risk management primarily used to hedge against the risk of a contingent loss. _____ is defined as the equitable transfer of the risk of a loss, from one entity to another, in exchange for a premium, and can be thought of as a guaranteed small loss to prevent a large, possibly devastating loss. An insurer is a company selling the _____; an insured or policyholder is the person or entity buying the _____.
   a. ACCRA Cost of Living Index
   b. ACEA agreement
   c. Insurance
   d. AD-IA Model

12. In microeconomics, the reservation (or reserve) price is the maximum price a buyer is willing to pay for a good or service; or, conversely, the minimum price at which a seller is willing to sell a good or service. _____s are commonly used in auctions.

_____s vary for the buyer according to their disposable income, their desire for the good, and the prices of, and their information about substitute goods.

a. Producer surplus
c. Returns to scale
b. Reservation price
d. Mohring effect

13. _____ are conceptually similar to economies of scale. Whereas economies of scale primarily refer to efficiencies associated with supply-side changes, such as increasing or decreasing the scale of production, of a single product type, _____ refer to efficiencies primarily associated with demand-side changes, such as increasing or decreasing the scope of marketing and distribution, of different types of products. _____ are one of the main reasons for such marketing strategies as product bundling, product lining, and family branding.

a. Economies of scale
c. Economic production quantity
b. Isoquant
d. Economies of scope

14. _____s are American state laws that provide a remedy for purchasers of cars that repeatedly fail to meet standards of quality and performance. These cars are called lemons. The federal _____ protects citizens of all states.

a. Lemon law
c. High-reeve
b. No Child Left Behind
d. Celler-Kefauver Act

15. _____ is the area of law in which manufacturers, distributors, suppliers, retailers, and others who make products available to the public are held responsible for the injuries those products cause.

In the United States, the claims most commonly associated with _____ are negligence, strict liability, breach of warranty, and various consumer protection claims. The majority of _____ laws are determined at the state level and vary widely from state to state.

a. 100-year flood
c. 130-30 fund
b. 1921 recession
d. Product liability

16. The _____ consists of a number of economic theories which describe the nature of the firm, company including its existence, its behaviour, and its relationship with the market.

In simplified terms, the _____ aims to answer these questions:

1. Existence - why do firms emerge, why are not all transactions in the economy mediated over the market?
2. Boundaries - why the boundary between firms and the market is located exactly there? Which transactions are performed internally and which are negotiated on the market?
3. Organization - why are firms structured in such specific way? What is the interplay of formal and informal relationships?

Despite looking simple, these questions are not answered by the established economic theory, which usually views firms as given, and treats them as black boxes without any internal structure.

Chapter 19. Asymmetric Information

The First World War period saw a change of emphasis in economic theory away from industry-level analysis which mainly included analysing markets to analysis at the level of the firm, as it became increasingly clear that perfect competition was no longer an adequate model of how firms behaved. Economic theory till then had focussed on trying to understand markets alone and there had been little study on understanding why firms or organisations exist.

a. Technology gap
b. Khazzoom-Brookes postulate
c. Theory of the firm
d. Policy Ineffectiveness Proposition

17. _____ is a specific term used in companies' financial reporting from the company-whole point of view. Because that use excludes the effects of changing ownership interest, an economic measure of _____ is necessary for financial analysis from the shareholders' point of view

_____ is defined by the Financial Accounting Standards Board, or FASB, as e;the change in equity [net assets] of a business enterprise during a period from transactions and other events and circumstances from nonowner sources. It includes all changes in equity during a period except those resulting from investments by owners and distributions to owners.e;

_____ is the sum of net income and other items that must bypass the income statement because they have not been realized, including items like an unrealized holding gain or loss from available for sale securities and foreign currency translation gains or losses.

a. Net national income
b. Real income
c. Windfall gain
d. Comprehensive income

18. _____ is one of the four Ps of the marketing mix. The other three aspects are product, promotion, and place. It is also a key variable in microeconomic price allocation theory.

a. Pricing
b. Guaranteed Maximum Price
c. Point of total assumption
d. Premium pricing

19. The _____, a unit of the United States Department of Labor, is the principal fact-finding agency for the U.S. government in the broad field of labor economics and statistics. The BLS is an independent national statistical agency that collects, processes, analyzes, and disseminates essential statistical data to the American public, the U.S. Congress, other Federal agencies, State and local governments, business, and labor representatives. The BLS also serves as a statistical resource to the Department of Labor.

a. Gross world product
b. Gross Regional Product
c. Bureau of Labor Statistics
d. Gross national product

Chapter 20. Contracts and Moral Hazards

1. _____ is the prospect that a party insulated from risk may behave differently from the way it would behave if it were fully exposed to the risk. In insurance, _____ that occurs without conscious or malicious action is called morale hazard.

   _____ is related to information asymmetry, a situation in which one party in a transaction has more information than another.

   a. 1921 recession
   b. Moral hazard
   c. 100-year flood
   d. 130-30 fund

2. _____, anti-selection insurance, statistics, and risk management. It refers to a market process in which 'bad' results occur when buyers and sellers have asymmetric information (i.e. access to different information): the 'bad' products or customers are more likely to be selected. A bank that sets one price for all its checking account customers runs the risk of being adversely selected against by its low-balance, high-activity (and hence least profitable) customers.
   a. ACEA agreement
   b. Adverse selection
   c. AD-IA Model
   d. ACCRA Cost of Living Index

3. _____ in economics refers to metrics and measures of output from production processes, per unit of input. Labor _____, for example, is typically measured as a ratio of output per labor-hour, an input. _____ may be conceived of as a metrics of the technical or engineering efficiency of production.
   a. Production-possibility frontier
   b. Fordism
   c. Piece work
   d. Productivity

4. _____ is a fee paid on borrowed assets. It is the price paid for the use of borrowed money, or, money earned by deposited funds. Assets that are sometimes lent with _____ include money, shares, consumer goods through hire purchase, major assets such as aircraft, and even entire factories in finance lease arrangements.
   a. Asset protection
   b. Internal debt
   c. Insolvency
   d. Interest

5. An _____ is the price a borrower pays for the use of money they do not own, for instance a small company might borrow from a bank to kick start their business, and the return a lender receives for deferring the use of funds, by lending it to the borrower. _____s are normally expressed as a percentage rate over the period of one year.

   _____s targets are also a vital tool of monetary policy and are used to control variables like investment, inflation, and unemployment.

   a. Arrow-Debreu model
   b. ACCRA Cost of Living Index
   c. Enterprise value
   d. Interest rate

6. _____ is a branch of economics that studies how individuals, households and firms and some states make decisions to allocate limited resources, typically in markets where goods or services are being bought and sold. _____ examines how these decisions and behaviours affect the supply and demand for goods and services, which determines prices; and how prices, in turn, determine the supply and demand of goods and services.

   Whereas macroeconomics involves the 'sum total of economic activity, dealing with the issues of growth, inflation and unemployment, and with national economic policies relating to these issues' and the effects of government actions on them.

Chapter 20. Contracts and Moral Hazards

a. Microeconomics
c. New Keynesian economics
b. Countercyclical
d. Recession

7. In political science and economics, the _____ or agency dilemma treats the difficulties that arise under conditions of incomplete and asymmetric information when a principal hires an agent, such as the problem that the two may not have the same interests, while the principal is, presumably, hiring the agent to pursue the interests of the former.

Various mechanisms may be used to try to align the interests of the agent with those of the principal, such as piece rates/commissions, profit sharing, efficiency wages, performance measurement (including financial statements), the agent posting a bond, or fear of firing. The _____ is found in most employer/employee relationships, for example, when stockholders hire top executives of corporations.

a. 100-year flood
c. 1921 recession
b. 130-30 fund
d. Principal-agent problem

8. In microeconomics, _____ is quite simply the conversion of inputs into outputs. It is an economic process that uses resources to create a good or service that is suitable for exchange. This can include manufacturing, storing, shipping, and packaging.
a. Production
c. Solved
b. Red Guards
d. MET

9. A _____ is a situation that involves losing one quality or aspect of something in return for gaining another quality or aspect. It implies a decision to be made with full comprehension of both the upside and downside of a particular choice.

In economics the term is expressed as opportunity cost, referring the most preferred alternative given up.

a. Trade-off
c. Nonmarket
b. Whitemail
d. Friedman-Savage utility function

10. In finance, a _____ is a debt security, in which the authorized issuer owes the holders a debt and, depending on the terms of the _____, is obliged to pay interest (the coupon) and/or to repay the principal at a later date, termed maturity. A _____ is a formal contract to repay borrowed money with interest at fixed intervals.

Thus a _____ is like a loan: the issuer is the borrower (debtor), the holder is the lender (creditor), and the coupon is the interest.

a. Callable
c. Bond
b. Prize Bond
d. Zero-coupon

11. _____s is the social science that studies the production, distribution, and consumption of goods and services. The term _____s comes from the Ancient Greek οἰκονομῑα from οἶκος (oikos, 'house') + νόμος (nomos, 'custom' or 'law'), hence 'rules of the house(hold)'. Current _____ models developed out of the broader field of political economy in the late 19th century, owing to a desire to use an empirical approach more akin to the physical sciences.
a. Inflation
c. Economic
b. Opportunity cost
d. Energy economics

12. A _____ is the transfer of wealth from one party (such as a person or company) to another. A _____ is usually made in exchange for the provision of goods, services or both, or to fulfill a legal obligation.

The simplest and oldest form of _____ is barter, the exchange of one good or service for another.

   a. Going concern
   c. Social gravity
   b. Soft count
   d. Payment

13. In economics, an _____ is any good (e.g. a commodity) or service brought into one country from another country in a legitimate fashion, typically for use in trade. It is a good that is brought in from another country for sale. _____ goods or services are provided to domestic consumers by foreign producers. An _____ in the receiving country is an export to the sending country.

   a. Incoterms
   c. Import
   b. Import quota
   d. Economic integration

14. In economics and sociology, an _____ is any factor (financial or non-financial) that enables or motivates a particular course of action, or counts as a reason for preferring one choice to the alternatives. It is an expectation that encourages people to behave in a certain way. Since human beings are purposeful creatures, the study of _____ structures is central to the study of all economic activity (both in terms of individual decision-making and in terms of co-operation and competition within a larger institutional structure.)

   a. Epstein-Zin preferences
   c. Isocost
   b. Economic reform
   d. Incentive

15. The _____ of a decision depends on both the cost of the alternative chosen and the benefit that the best alternative would have provided if chosen. _____ differs from accounting cost because it includes opportunity cost.

   a. Epstein-Zin preferences
   c. Inventory analysis
   b. Isocost
   d. Economic cost

16. Under the system of feudalism, a _____, fief, feud, feoff often consisted of inheritable lands or revenue-producing property granted by a liege lord, generally to a vassal, in return for a form of allegiance, originally to give him the means to fulfill his military duties when called upon. However anything of value could be held in fief, such as an office, a right of exploitation (e.g., hunting, fishing) or any other type of revenue, rather than the land it comes from.

Originally, the feudal institution of vassalage did not imply the giving or receiving of landholdings (which were granted only as a reward for loyalty), but by the eighth century the giving of a landholding was becoming standard.

   a. 1921 recession
   c. 100-year flood
   b. 130-30 fund
   d. Fiefdom

17. In options, the _____ is a key variable in a derivatives contract between two parties. Where the contract requires delivery of the underlying instrument, the trade will be at the _____, regardless of the spot price (market price) of the underlying instrument at that time.

Definition - The fixed price at which the owner of an option can purchase, in the case of a call in the case of a put, the underlying security or commodity.

a. Binary option
c. Calendar spread
b. Married put
d. Strike price

18. _____ are a system of financial incentives designed to keep an employee from leaving the company. These can include employee stock options which will not vest for several years but are more often contractual obligations to give back lucrative bonuses or other compensation if the employee leaves for another company.

_____ are a response by the companies in industries where it is common for highly compensated employees to frequently move from one firm to another, often before the company feels that it has earned a return on the investment in the employee.

a. Procurement
c. Golden hello
b. Small business
d. Golden handcuffs

19. _____ in economics and business is the result of an exchange and from that trade we assign a numerical monetary value to a good, service or asset. If Alice trades Bob 4 apples for an orange, the _____ of an orange is 4 apples. Inversely, the _____ of an apple is 1/4 oranges.

a. Premium pricing
c. Price book
b. Price war
d. Price

20. _____ exists when sales of identical goods or services are transacted at different prices from the same provider. In a theoretical market with perfect information, no transaction costs or prohibition on secondary exchange (or re-selling) to prevent arbitrage, _____ can only be a feature of monopoly and oligopoly markets, where market power can be exercised. Otherwise, the moment the seller tries to sell the same good at different prices, the buyer at the lower price can arbitrage by selling to the consumer buying at the higher price but with a tiny discount.

a. Lerner Index
c. Loss leader
b. Transfer pricing
d. Price discrimination

21. In labor economics, the _____ hypothesis argues that wages, at least in some markets, are determined by more than simply supply and demand. Specifically, it points to the incentive for managers to pay their employees more than the market-clearing wage in order to increase their productivity or efficiency. This increased labor productivity pays for the relatively higher wages.

a. Exogenous growth model
c. Earnings calls
b. Inflatable rats
d. Efficiency wage

22. _____ are conceptually similar to economies of scale. Whereas economies of scale primarily refer to efficiencies associated with supply-side changes, such as increasing or decreasing the scale of production, of a single product type, _____ refer to efficiencies primarily associated with demand-side changes, such as increasing or decreasing the scope of marketing and distribution, of different types of products. _____ are one of the main reasons for such marketing strategies as product bundling, product lining, and family branding.

a. Economies of scale
c. Economies of scope
b. Isoquant
d. Economic production quantity

23. A _____ association is a financial institution that specializes in accepting savings deposits and making mortgage and other loans. The S'L or thrift term is mainly used in the United States; similar institutions in the United Kingdom, Ireland and some Commonwealth countries include building societies and trustee savings banks.

They are often mutually held, meaning that the depositors and borrowers are members with voting rights, and have the ability to direct the financial and managerial goals of the organization, similar to the policyholders of a mutual insurance company.

a. Fonds commun de placement
b. Collective investment scheme
c. Participating policy
d. Savings and loan

24. The phrase _____ and acquisitions refers to the aspect of corporate strategy, corporate finance and management dealing with the buying, selling and combining of different companies that can aid, finance, or help a growing company in a given industry grow rapidly without having to create another business entity.

An acquisition, also known as a takeover or a buyout, is the buying of one company (the 'target') by another. An acquisition may be friendly or hostile.

a. Mergers
b. Differential accumulation
c. Peace dividend
d. Political economy

ANSWER KEY

Chapter 1
1. a   2. d   3. a   4. a   5. d   6. a   7. d   8. c   9. c   10. d
11. d   12. b   13. b   14. d   15. b   16. a   17. d   18. d   19. d   20. d
21. d   22. d

Chapter 2
1. d   2. d   3. a   4. b   5. d   6. d   7. d   8. d   9. d   10. d
11. d   12. d   13. d   14. b   15. d   16. c   17. d   18. b   19. d   20. d
21. d   22. b   23. a   24. d   25. b   26. d   27. d   28. c   29. a   30. c
31. d   32. b   33. d   34. c

Chapter 3
1. c   2. a   3. c   4. d   5. c   6. d   7. c   8. d   9. a   10. c
11. d   12. b   13. c   14. d   15. d   16. c   17. b   18. d   19. d   20. d
21. b   22. d   23. b   24. b   25. d   26. d   27. a   28. d   29. a   30. d
31. b

Chapter 4
1. d   2. d   3. c   4. c   5. d   6. a   7. d   8. a   9. d   10. d
11. d   12. c   13. a   14. d   15. c   16. d   17. c   18. b   19. c   20. c
21. b   22. d   23. a   24. b

Chapter 5
1. c   2. d   3. d   4. a   5. a   6. b   7. b   8. d   9. d   10. a
11. b   12. a   13. a   14. d   15. a   16. d   17. b   18. a   19. b   20. d
21. d   22. d   23. a   24. d   25. b   26. b   27. b   28. d   29. d   30. d
31. c   32. d   33. d   34. c   35. d   36. b   37. d   38. b   39. d   40. d
41. d   42. d   43. d   44. b   45. b   46. c   47. d   48. d

Chapter 6
1. d   2. c   3. d   4. d   5. b   6. a   7. d   8. a   9. a   10. c
11. d   12. d   13. d   14. c   15. d   16. d   17. a   18. d   19. a   20. c
21. d   22. d   23. d   24. a   25. a   26. c   27. d   28. a   29. d   30. d
31. c   32. d   33. a   34. d

Chapter 7
1. d   2. d   3. d   4. d   5. d   6. c   7. c   8. a   9. d   10. b
11. c   12. d   13. c   14. d   15. c   16. d   17. d   18. d   19. d   20. d
21. d   22. c   23. c   24. c   25. d   26. c   27. d   28. d   29. d   30. a
31. d   32. c   33. b   34. a   35. c   36. d   37. c   38. c   39. c   40. d
41. d   42. d   43. a   44. c   45. d   46. c   47. d   48. a   49. d

Chapter 8

1. b	2. b	3. c	4. d	5. d	6. c	7. c	8. b	9. d	10. c
11. d	12. c	13. d	14. d	15. d	16. c	17. d	18. c	19. c	20. d
21. d	22. c	23. c	24. c	25. b	26. d	27. c	28. a	29. b	30. b
31. d	32. d	33. a	34. a	35. c	36. d	37. c	38. d	39. c	40. c
41. a	42. c	43. c	44. b						

Chapter 9

1. d	2. a	3. a	4. d	5. c	6. c	7. b	8. a	9. d	10. a
11. d	12. d	13. d	14. d	15. b	16. b	17. d	18. a	19. b	20. a
21. c	22. d	23. d	24. d	25. d	26. d	27. d	28. d	29. c	30. d
31. c	32. b	33. b	34. a	35. d	36. b	37. a	38. b	39. a	40. d
41. d	42. d	43. d	44. d	45. d	46. a	47. a	48. a	49. d	50. d

Chapter 10

1. a	2. b	3. b	4. d	5. d	6. d	7. d	8. d	9. b	10. d
11. d	12. a	13. b	14. b	15. d	16. d	17. d	18. d	19. a	20. d
21. a	22. d	23. c	24. d	25. d	26. d	27. a	28. d	29. c	30. d
31. d	32. d	33. a	34. c	35. d	36. b	37. b	38. a	39. c	40. d
41. d	42. d	43. a	44. c	45. c	46. d	47. d			

Chapter 11

1. b	2. d	3. d	4. b	5. a	6. a	7. c	8. b	9. d	10. a
11. a	12. d	13. d	14. d	15. d	16. d	17. a	18. d	19. b	20. a
21. d	22. b	23. d	24. b	25. d	26. b	27. d	28. a	29. d	30. d
31. d	32. d	33. d	34. a	35. a	36. c	37. d	38. d	39. d	40. a
41. d	42. c	43. b	44. c	45. a	46. b				

Chapter 12

1. b	2. c	3. b	4. b	5. c	6. b	7. d	8. a	9. d	10. b
11. b	12. a	13. b	14. b	15. a	16. d	17. c	18. c	19. a	20. c
21. c	22. d	23. a	24. a	25. d	26. d	27. c			

Chapter 13

1. d	2. d	3. c	4. d	5. b	6. a	7. d	8. d	9. d	10. c
11. a	12. d	13. d	14. d	15. d	16. d	17. b	18. a	19. b	20. d
21. d	22. a	23. d	24. a	25. c	26. a	27. d	28. c	29. d	30. d
31. d	32. b	33. c	34. d	35. d	36. d	37. b	38. c	39. c	40. d
41. d	42. c	43. d	44. d	45. b	46. d	47. b	48. d	49. d	50. d
51. d	52. a	53. c	54. d	55. c					

ANSWER KEY

Chapter 14
1. d   2. d   3. c   4. a   5. b   6. a   7. d   8. d   9. b   10. d
11. c   12. a   13. b   14. d   15. d   16. d   17. c   18. c   19. d   20. c
21. d   22. d   23. b   24. d   25. b

Chapter 15
1. d   2. a   3. d   4. d   5. c   6. d   7. d   8. a   9. d   10. d
11. b   12. c   13. d   14. c   15. a   16. a   17. d   18. d   19. d   20. b
21. d   22. c   23. d   24. b   25. d   26. b   27. b   28. d   29. d   30. a
31. a   32. c   33. a   34. d   35. d   36. d   37. c   38. d   39. c   40. a
41. d

Chapter 16
1. d   2. c   3. d   4. c   5. a   6. b   7. d   8. b   9. c   10. c
11. d   12. d   13. a   14. a   15. c   16. c   17. d   18. d   19. d   20. d
21. c   22. c   23. b   24. d   25. b   26. c   27. d   28. a   29. b   30. d
31. c   32. d   33. a   34. d   35. d   36. d   37. a   38. d   39. d   40. a
41. d   42. a   43. b   44. d   45. d

Chapter 17
1. c   2. c   3. d   4. c   5. a   6. d   7. d   8. a   9. a   10. a
11. a   12. d   13. a   14. d   15. c   16. b   17. c   18. c   19. d   20. d
21. d

Chapter 18
1. d   2. a   3. d   4. a   5. d   6. d   7. b   8. d   9. d   10. a
11. a   12. d   13. a   14. c   15. a   16. b   17. b   18. d   19. d   20. b
21. d   22. b   23. d   24. b   25. d   26. d   27. b   28. b   29. b   30. d
31. c   32. d   33. c   34. c   35. d   36. d   37. d   38. a   39. c   40. a
41. d   42. c   43. d   44. b   45. d   46. d   47. d

Chapter 19
1. d   2. d   3. a   4. a   5. a   6. b   7. b   8. c   9. b   10. d
11. c   12. b   13. d   14. a   15. d   16. c   17. d   18. a   19. c

Chapter 20
1. b   2. b   3. d   4. d   5. d   6. a   7. d   8. a   9. a   10. c
11. c   12. d   13. c   14. d   15. d   16. d   17. d   18. d   19. d   20. d
21. d   22. c   23. d   24. a